EMPIRICAL PERSPECTIVES OF CELEBRITY ENDORSEMENTS

Dr. Kisholoy Roy

© Kisholoy Roy

First edition: 2018

ISBN: 9781982934323

Copyright of this book solely rests with the author and no part of this book shall be reproduced or transmitted in any form across any medium without the consent of the author

Preface

This book titled ***Empirical Perspectives of Celebrity Endorsements*** is a collection of some of the best empirical research papers that i have developed for over a decade in the area of celebrity endorsements.

This book starts off with the introduction to the subject of celebrity endorsements which is extremely relevant and interesting in contemporary era since a lot of paradigm shifts and emerging practices have come to the fore in the last couple of years in the business of brands and brand communication.

This book mainly emphasizes on celebrity endorsements across product categories and their respective contributions in terms of effects and impacts.

The book signs off with two crucial chapters in the form of research papers – one on how the effects of endorsements and endorser types differ/do not differ across product categories and the consumer perceptions regarding outcomes of celebrity endorsements in general.

This is book is entirely research based and hence any research scholar working in this area will stand to gain good amount of fodder to seek direction and further his research in the domain of celebrity endorsements.

- **Dr Kisholoy Roy**

Contents

An Introduction to Celebrity Endorsements   9-21

Celebrity Endorsements & Altered Brand Gendering   22-69

Celebrity Endorsements & Sports Marketing   70-97

Celebrity Endorsements and Men's Intimate Wear   98-115

Celebrity Endorsements & Industrial Products   116-138

Celebrity Endorser Types & Product Categories   139-171

The Perceived Outcomes of Celebrity Endorsements   172-192

An Introduction to Celebrity Endorsements

Who is a celebrity? Why does a company or for that matter a brand require a celebrity? Do they really aid a brand at any stage of a brand's life cycle? Do all products require a celebrity? What are the pros and cons associated with a celebrity? How to go about selecting a celebrity for a brand? What is celebrity endorsement? What are the contributors for effective celebrity endorsements? Are celebrity endorsements a decorated shield for lack of creative ideas for a brand? Do celebrity endorsements guarantee extra bucks for a brand in terms of sales? How do celebrity endorsements affect the bottom line of a company? These and a number of other questions will be answered in this first and the subsequent chapters of this book.

Media vehicles in today's world are simply clogged with plethora of advertisements of various brands because of which it is difficult for a brand to get noticed and being tried by the potential consumer. It is a difficult task thus for the developers of advertising campaign to differentiate a brand within the media clutter and attract the attention of potential customers. In the present age of marketing communication, it has often been noticed that audiences and readers consciously try to evade advertisements while flipping through newspapers or magazines or while they are listening to radio or watching television. It is due to this reason that many marketers have adopted the strategy of celebrity endorsements for brands which is a form of differentiated communication and is of great significance for brands being advertised.

Modern day marketing is no more about transaction selling but of relationship marketing which requires suitable understanding of the repeat purchase behaviour of customers. This understanding is required while introducing celebrities for brand communications in order to create strong brand affiliations among the customers. The image of the endorsers has a direct impact on the image of the product being advertised as customers are often found to relate the celebrities to the products being advertised and although the success of endorsers in inducing sales is considered to be high; rarely are their impact on brands measured in terms of repeat sales when it comes to marketing practice.

Over the years, marketers have been found to make all possible efforts in promoting brands and grab the mind share of customers. Marketers have been found to introduce celebrities in advertisements through testimonials, endorsements, as actors or as a spokesperson for some brand. Celebrity endorsement as an exercise works well for products with high price-production cost margin and large customer base. In other words, they are more suited for nationally marketed brands than for locally marketed ones. There are certain product categories that need to reach out to multiple customer groups and here again celebrity endorsements have been found to be an effective strategy. Marketers need to decide how far returns outweigh the risks associated with taking a celebrity for an advertisement. The appeal of a celebrity needs to be suitably blended with the image of the brand so that marketers can reap benefits out of an endorsement. While endorsements serve as an aid to brand recall and influence brand purchases, they can also become a nightmare for marketers if the endorsement is not backed by a powerful idea and suitable positioning.

In the contemporary marketing arena, celebrity endorsements have been considered as a preferred tool of advertising by several marketers and have been largely perceived as a winning formula for both product marketing and brand building. For marketers, it's a challenge to establish a strong association between a product and a celebrity because at the end of the day it endorsements are aimed at building brands and not build celebrities. There are certain pros and cons of endorsements. Some of the reasons why marketers go for celebrities are quick saliency, quick connect, quick means of brand differentiation and credibility. As far as drawbacks of celebrity endorsements are concerned, celebrity overshadowing a brand, celebrity trap and celebrity clutter are some to be mentioned. There is a 14 point model that serves as a guideline for marketers to go for celebrity endorsements in an effective manner. The contents of the model are celebrity profession, celebrity physical attractiveness, celebrity values, celebrity availability, cost of acquiring celebrity, celebrity regional appeal, celebrity credibility, fit with the advertising idea, whether celebrity is a brand user, multiple endorsements, celebrity controversy risk, celebrity product match, celebrity target audience match and celebrity popularity. Marketers need to get rid of the perception that they can control everything related to the brand if they have a celebrity to endorse it. They need to see if the celebrity associates well with the brand and can actually enhance the acceptance of the brand among its target audience.

Companies largely adopt celebrity endorsements as marketing strategy for the purpose of supporting corporate or brand imagery. They have been found to juxtapose brands or organizations with endorser qualities like attractiveness, likeability and trustworthiness as they opine that these operate in a transferable way and generate desirable campaign outcomes. There are times when celebrity qualities are inappropriate and irrelevant apart from being undesirable and under such circumstances celebrity endorsements turn a liability for advertisers. Certain factors need to be considered during the celebrity selection process to enhance the effectiveness of endorsements.

Celebrity endorsements are no different than other form of advertising as because it is driven by an idea and if the idea works well with the target audience, the endorsement will work too else it is doomed to be a failure. The effectiveness of the technique is based on the fact that consumers often tend to feel that if a celebrity of their liking endorses a product then, it is the right product for them. Celebrity endorsement as a strategy is not just restricted to B2C markets but it has often been adopted in B2B advertising as well. Companies operating in the B2B sphere are found to use customer referencing as a tool for promoting products but then at times they are also found to go for prominent individuals for promoting their products. One important observation when it comes to endorsements in B2B markets is that instead of individuals who are celebrities because of their performance in the field of sports or entertainment, the personalities being used have high profiles because of their extraordinary success in leading organizations in one or a number of product sectors or by way of their success in championing a particular cause.

The high costs associated with product advertising require advertisers to adopt measures that enhance the interests of consumers in products. Advertisers are required to put in more efforts in going for endorsers who gel with a brand and also create endorsements that provide strong arguments and believable explanations regarding why endorsers truly like the product they endorse. Repeat purchase is an important element of the marketing concept and this is actually supported by celebrity endorsements. It needs to be understood that how consumers respond and relate to celebrities across product categories. Researches have revealed that celebrity endorsers are mostly males rather than females, around 30 years of age and they are generally from the world of entertainment. The product categories they are mostly found to endorse are clothing and shoes, cosmetics, personal care and hygiene products. It has been further observed that celebrities do not participate in testimonials as such. Another important observation regarding celebrity endorsements is that endorsements mostly happen more for low involvement products rather than high involvement products.

Celebrity endorsement as a marketing strategy has become quite prominent as a brand promotion technique in contemporary India due to the emerging integrated marketing communication concept. The emergence of modern day endorsements happened in the 1980s and since then the beauty products and the fragrance brands have been found to consistently associate with celebrities to market themselves. Pursuing celebrity endorsements enables advertisers to project credible image in terms of expertise, persuasiveness, trustworthiness and objectiveness.

It can be well said that celebrity endorsement is no magic wand for companies to be waved and it will start working magic for brands. A carefully thought endorsement plot, a suitable celebrity-product match and a suitable celebrity-target audience match, a suitable celebrity-brand profile match are some basic ingredients besides of course a number of factors that ensure a celebrity endorsement favouring brand sales.

Endorsements & Altered Brand Gendering

1.0 Introduction

Sample the following facts:

- A Gillette India survey conducted on Indian men and women revealed that Indian men on an average spend 20 minutes in the mirror each morning compared to 18-minute average for Indian women

- A survey by New Delhi-based retail consultancy firm KSA Technopak revealed that 70% of urban Indian males visit a salon at least once a month

- Of about 70,000 salons in the country's top 100 cities, about 60% thrive by catering only to men
- The men's grooming market is estimated at $2billion and is growing annually at a rate of 20%
- Men's fairness products market is estimated at $40 million and is growing annually at a rate of 25% while women's fairness market is growing at a rate of 7%-8%.

The above facts clearly indicate one aspect of Indian males and that is looking good which was a matter of feeling good earlier has become a necessity for them. A large cross section of Indian male populace believe that being well groomed is the key to not just a bright professional career but also other bright prospects in one's life. Since the dawn of the 21st century, a particular term has been frequently used to describe the Indian urban men and that is 'metrosexual' which is to describe all those men who believe that looking good and well groomed is an integral part of one's overall personality. In the contemporary era, it has been observed that men of all ages have taken a keen interest in their appearance. While the youth have gone for grooming products that can prolong their youthful charm and aura, the older men folk have resorted to products that have anti-ageing qualities. Based on the clientele profile of 45 clinics of Kaya Skin care across the country, it was found that men older than 60 have frequently visited the clinics for radical improvement in their appearance.

The above mentioned trend has been found to propel many marketers in the country to launch grooming products exclusively for men. Men's grooming products mainly include face wash, deodorants, face cleansers, moisturizers, hair gels, body wash, fairness creams and shaving products. Gillette is one brand that leads the men's grooming category courtesy its shaving range that offers the company 31% overall value share in the market. One significant observation made by many marketers is that Indian men are far more discerning than their women counterparts. While for women, it is all about pampering them well, for men, they believe in results. A brand not delivering on the promise cannot seek loyalty of the male clientele.

An interesting observation in the context of launching grooming products for men is that many brands that originally catered to the grooming requirements of women and were perceived by and large to be feminine have customized their products, packaging and communication strategies with the objective of claiming a chunk of the lucrative and promising male grooming market. L'Oreal, the global cosmetics company that reportedly sold grooming products exclusively for Indian women for years and communicated in the mass media mainly through celebrities like Aishwarya Rai Bachchan and Penelope Cruz introduced three products from its international range for Indian men that included anti-fatigue creams, hydrating gels and anti-wrinkle creams and cleansers. Similarly Emami launched the Fair & Handsome fairness cream for Indian men. Garnier, another global cosmetics brand launched Men's Powerlight range that included face wash and moisturizer. Vaseline mainly known as a brand to relieve cracked lips during winters and used mostly by women also launched products like face creams and face wash for men with Bollywood star Shahid Kapur as the brand's endorser.

It needs to be studied that how the above mentioned customizations have impacted the overall understanding of the brands from the consumer's perspective, the brand perception, general acceptability of the brands and consumer's purchase intention of the brands. For the purpose of study five brands (related to grooming) have been considered viz. L'Oreal, Fiama Di Wills, Garnier, Emami and Vaseline.

2.0 Literature Review

One of the major objectives of positioning strategies is to associate brands with masculine or feminine personality traits. It has been widely observed that consumers draw on these gender dimensions of brand personality to enhance their own degree of masculinity or femininity when they consume brands for self-expressive purposes. Brand gendering as a technique has been found to be especially relevant for brands that have a symbolic connotation for consumers. Marketers have generally been found to use personality scales developed for the assessment of human personality traits to measure gender dimensions of brand personality. However the efficacy of using such scales for the above mentioned purpose has been highly questionable. To enhance the objectivity of measurement of gender dimensions of brand personality a series of eight studies were conducted to develop and validate a two-dimensional scale measuring masculine and feminine brand personality (Grohmann, 2009). The two-dimensional scale was found to be applicable to both utilitarian and symbolic brands across a range of product categories.

Basically, functional and attribute orientation has served as the platform for product positioning while emotional associations have been the key to brand positioning. Brand gendering has been utilized as a tool by marketers to create strong differentiation for brands in the market place and has been simply defined as the process of associating a brand with a particular gender (Panda, 2006). There are certain guidelines to be followed and caveats to be aware of as far using the technique of brand gendering is concerned. There are various strategic alternatives of gendering a brand which generally have a long term impact on brands.

Brand gendering has been described as associating the image of a brand with a sex role stereotype in the minds of consumers (Alreck, 1994). In-depth research has been conducted to evaluate the requirements and prohibitions of contemporary masculine and feminine sex roles and the kinds of consumers who do and do not adhere to them. There are certain guidelines for choosing an appropriate brand gendering strategy based on target market demographics and the tendency of different customer segments to prefer gendered brands over the un-gendered ones.

Although extensive studies have been conducted detailing conceptual framework of brand gendering and the guidelines involved in implementing effective brand gendering strategies, no such study has been conducted especially in the Indian context where by customization of a gendered brand for the opposite sex has been detailed. Such customization is expected to have an influence on the overall brand personality, customer perception and brand acceptability, and purchase intention of customers. There is a need to study the impact that customization of gendered brands have on consumer psyche and on brands.

3.0 Research Objectives

- To analyze the general consumer perception of the brands under study viz. L'Oreal, Fiama Di Wills, Garnier, Emami and Vaseline
- To evaluate consumers' gender perception of the brands under study viz. L'Oreal, Fiama Di Wills, Garnier, Emami and Vaseline
- To analyze the level of consumer awareness regarding the availability of

the Men's range of the brands under study

- To analyze if the awareness regarding the availability of the Men's range of the brands under study have an influence on consumers' perceptions regarding the brand

- To understand if the awareness regarding the availability of the Men's range of the brands under study have an influence on the acceptability of the brands

- To evaluate if the awareness regarding the availability of the Men's range of the brands under study have an influence on consumers' purchase intention of the brands

4.0 Research Hypotheses

H1: There is no significant difference between the perceived genders (Male, Female and Neutral) of the brands under study

H2: There is no significant difference between the genders of informants and their perception regarding a brand's gender

H3: There is no significant difference between the genders of informants and their level of awareness regarding the availability of Men's range of the brands under study

H4: There is no influence of the gender of informants and their level of awareness regarding availability of men's range of the brands studied on the overall perception of the brands

H5: There is no influence of the gender of informants and their level of awareness regarding availability of men's range of the brands studied on brand acceptability

H6: There is no influence of the gender of informants and their level of awareness regarding availability of men's range of the brands studied on consumers' purchase intentions of the brands

5.0 Research Design

There is an independent variable and several dependent variables in the study.

5.1 Variables

5.1.1 Independent Variable: Communication mix of the brands under study

5.1.2 Dependent Variables: General consumer perception of the brands, Gender perceptions of the brands from the consumer's perspective, Consumers' acceptability of the brands, Consumers' purchase intention of the brands

5.2 Sample Size: 50 individuals in the age bracket of 25-45 years were surveyed. Most of the respondents were students of the MBA program while the rest of the informants were teachers, research scholars or professionals. Of the 50 individuals surveyed, 28 were Female while 22 were

Male. Most of the informants reported an annual family income that ranged from 3 lakhs to 5 lakhs.

5.3 Sampling Type: A combination of Judgmental and Convenience sampling was used to select the informants for the study

5.4 Data Collection: A structured Questionnaire was used to collect data. Data was sourced mostly from the Kolkata market through personal interview method. Some responses were sourced from outside the Kolkata market through email.

6.0 Research Findings

The survey revealed certain interesting findings regarding the overall perception of the gendered brands and the impact of customization strategies adopted by marketers for the women oriented brands considered for the study.

6.1 General Consumer Perceptions regarding the Brands under study

The informants for the survey were given a set of words like **Expensive, Exclusive, Premium, Affordable, Reliable, Nourishing, Rejuvenating, Reputed, Refreshing, Youthful, Aesthetic** and **Effective** that would best describe a particular brand considered for the survey. The words were shortlisted based on various perspectives related to the brands like price, brand name, product quality, brand performance and brand identity. Majority of the informants described L'Oreal as an expensive and an exclusive brand. Along with that words like reputed, premium and nourishing were also used. Majority of the respondents described Fiama Di Wills as a rejuvenating, refreshing and a youthful brand. Garnier was mostly described as a nourishing and a reliable brand. Emami was described as an affordable brand while Vaseline was described as a reliable, reputed and an effective brand. A suitable content analysis for each brand facilitated better and vivid understanding of the general customer perceptions of the brands under study **[Table 1.1(a-e)]**.

Table 1.1(a)
Content Analysis for L'Oreal

Referential	Propositional	Thematic
Price	Expensive	
Brand Name	Reputed, Reliable	A highly differentiated brand meant for premium customer segment
Product Quality	Premium, Exclusive	
Brand Performance	Nourishing, Rejuvenating, Effective	
Brand Identity	Youthful	

Table 1.1(b)
Content Analysis for Fiama Di Wills

Referential	Propositional	Thematic
Price	Affordable, Expensive	
Brand Name	Reputed	**Brand has an uninhibited appeal**
Product Quality	Premium, Exclusive	
Brand Performance	Rejuvenating, Refreshing, Effective	
Brand Identity	Youthful	

Table 1.1(c)
Content Analysis for Garnier

Referential	Propositional	Thematic
Price	Affordable, Expensive	
Brand Name	Reputed, Reliable	A trusted brand that reassures customer well being
Product Quality	Premium, Exclusive, Aesthetic	
Brand Performance	Nourishing, Rejuvenating, Effective, Refreshing	
Brand Identity	Youthful	

Table 1.1(d)
Content Analysis for Emami

Referential	Propositional	Thematic
Price	Affordable, Expensive	
Brand Name	Reputed, Reliable	A cost effective brand
Product Quality	Aesthetic	
Brand Performance	Nourishing, Refreshing, Effective	
Brand Identity	Youthful	

Table 1.1(e)
Content Analysis for Vaseline

Referential	Propositional	Thematic
Price	Affordable	
Brand Name	Reputed, Reliable	A trust worthy brand that delivers on its promise
Product Quality	Aesthetic, Premium, Exclusive	
Brand Performance	Nourishing, Rejuvenating, Effective	
Brand Identity	Youthful	

The content analysis for the brands under study revealed another important aspect related to the brands and that is all the brands were being perceived as catering to the youth. The respondents felt that the brands had a youth centric appeal.

6.2 Gender Perceptions of the Brands under study:

The informants were asked to assign a gender (Male, Female, Neutral) to each brand considered for the survey based on their perceptions. It was found that 94% of the informants assigned a feminine identity to L'Oreal while 54% of the respondents assigned a feminine gender to Fiama Di Wills. Garnier, Emami and Vaseline were mostly perceived as having a Neutral gender as was mentioned by 72% 74% and 78% of the respondents respectively. The need to find out any significant difference between the perceived genders of the brands under study was felt and for that a chi-square test was employed. . The calculated value of x^2 at 95% level of confidence and at d.f.(degrees of freedom)=8 is 87.94. **Since Table value of x^2 (15.5) < Calculated value of x^2 (87.94), it is proved that significant differences between the perceived genders of brands exist. H1, which states that there is no significant difference between the perceived genders (Male, Female and Neutral) of the brands under study thus stands rejected based on the chi-square test results.**

The next objective was to find out if gender perceptions of brands under study differed with the gender of respondents. A chi-square test was undertaken for each brand under study to confirm the same. Results of the chi-square test undertaken for each brand have been mentioned in [Table 1.2].

Table 1.2
Chi-square Test Results for Establishing Significant Difference between Genders of Informants and their Perception regarding a Brand's Gender

Brands	Male Respondents			Female Respondents			χ^2
	(M)	(F)	(N)	(M)	(F)	(N)	
L'Oreal	1	19	2	0	28	0	2.375
Fiama Di Wills	0	13	9	0	10	18	2.708
Garnier	0	6	16	1	7	20	0.373
Emami	4	3	15	0	6	22	3.445
Vaseline	0	5	17	0	6	22	0.011

The above table highlights the number of male and female respondents who have perceived the brands under study as Male (M), Female (F) or Neutral (N) and the corresponding chi-square value for each brand. The table value of x^2 at 95% level of confidence and at d.f. = 2 is 5.99. **Since none of the calculated values of chi-square mentioned in Table 1.2 is more than the table value, H2, which states that there is no significant difference between the genders of informants and their perception regarding a brand's gender, is acceptable.**

6.3 Awareness regarding availability of the Men's range of the brands under study:

Informants were asked if the perception regarding a brand's gender influenced their purchase decision to which 100% of the population sample answered in the affirmative. Respondents were further queried regarding their level of awareness as far as availability of the men's range of the brands under study was concerned. 76% of the respondents were 'Not Aware' about the availability of the men's range of L'Oreal. 42% of the respondents were 'Somewhat Aware' of the availability of products meant for men as far as Fiama Di Wills brand was concerned. In case of Garnier, Emami and Vaseline, 66%, 72% and 62% of the respondents were 'Fully

Aware' of the availability of the men's range of the brands mentioned. The need to find out whether there was any significant differences of responses within respondent categories or not was felt for which the *Goodness of Fit* test was employed for each individual brand. The responses of male and female respondents along with the results for the male and female respondent categories have been highlighted in **[Table 1.3 (a-b)]**.

Table 1.3 (a)
Goodness of Fit Results for Male Respondents to Establish Significant Difference between Genders of Informants and their Level of Awareness regarding men's range of the brands under Study

Brands	Fully Aware	Somewhat Aware	Not Aware	χ^2
L'Oreal	2	6	14	10.19
Fiama Di Wills	5	7	10	1.72
Garnier	12	10	0	3.94
Emami	14	6	2	10.18
Vaseline	13	6	3	7.18

Table 1.3 (b)
Goodness of Fit Results for Female Respondents to Establish Significant Difference between Genders of Informants and their Level of Awareness regarding men's range of the brands under Study

Brands	Fully Aware	Somewhat Aware	Not Aware	χ^2
L'Oreal	0	4	24	26.11
Fiama Di Wills	4	14	10	5.39
Garnier	21	6	1	23.23
Emami	22	6	0	18.39
Vaseline	18	6	4	12.29

The table value of χ^2 at 95% level of confidence and at d.f. = 2 is 5.99. When compared with the calculated values in the Table 1.3 (a-b), it is observed significant differences of responses exist among the male respondents as far as L'Oreal, Emami and Vaseline is concerned. Variation of responses is thus acceptable in these brands. For the female respondents, significant differences exist among them as far as L'Oreal, Garnier, Emami and Vaseline is concerned. Variation of responses is thus acceptable in these brands. Among both respondent categories, significant differences of responses do not exist for the Fiama Di Wills brand. The same is true for Garnier in the context of female respondents. **Based on the *Goodness of Fit* results, H3, which states that there is no significant difference between the genders of informants and their level of awareness regarding the availability of Men's range of the brands under study stands rejected.**

Those who have viewed the advertisements highlighting the men's range of the brands under study were asked to comment on the brand-celebrity fit. Celebrities like John Abraham, Shah Rukh Khan and Shahid Kapur have endorsed the men's range of Garnier, Emami and Vaseline respectively. 38% of the respondents referred to the brand-celebrity fit of Garnier-John Abraham as 'Good'. 32% of the respondents referred to Emami-Shah Rukh Khan advertisements as 'Good'. However majority of the female informants opined the combination of Emami and Shah Rukh Khan (endorsing Fair and Handsome fairness cream) as 'Poor'. 34% of the respondents referred to the brand-celebrity fit of Vaseline and Shahid Kapur as 'Good'. 48% of the respondents however felt that product placement would be a better way to promote the men's range of the brands under study than celebrity endorsements or advertisements having no celebrities.

6.4 Perception, Acceptability and Purchase Intention of brands

Informants for the survey were asked whether there awareness regarding the men's range of the brands under study would influence their overall perception, acceptability and purchase intention of the brands. In short, it was to be understood whether the awareness regarding the men's range would make any difference to them in terms of the overall brand perception, brand acceptability and consumer's purchase intention.

In the context of influence on overall perception regarding the brand, 63% of the male informants confirmed that they will be influenced while 54% of the female respondents responded otherwise. 77% of the male respondents confirmed that they will be influenced as far as brand acceptability parameter is concerned while 61% of the female respondents observed that availability of the men's range will not make any difference to them as far as brand acceptability is concerned. 69% of the male informants observed that availability of the men's range will influence their purchase intention while 71% of the female respondents confirmed that they will not be influenced in this context. Summarizing the results, it was found that overall 54% and 56% of the respondents would be influenced by the availability of the men's range in the context of overall brand perception and brand acceptability respectively while 54%

of the respondents would not be influenced in the context of purchase intention of the brands under study. A chi-square test was employed to test H4, H5 and H6.

For testing H4, the calculated value of chi-square was found to 1.468. The table value of chi-square at 95% level of confidence and at d.f= 1 is 3.84. **Since table value of x^2 (3.84) > calculated value of x^2 (1.468), H4, which states that there is no influence of the gender of informants and their level of awareness regarding availability of men's range of the brands studied** on the overall perception of the brands stands accepted.

The calculated value of x^2 for testing H5 was found to be 7.21. The table value as stated in the earlier paragraph is 3.84. **Since the table value of x^2 (3.84) < calculated value of x^2 (7.21), H5, which states that there is no influence of the gender of informants and their level of awareness regarding availability of men's range of the brands studied on brand acceptability stands rejected.**

The calculated value of x^2 for testing H6 was found to be 7.77. **Since the table value of x^2 (3.84) < calculated value of x^2 (7.77), H6, which states that there is no influence of the gender of informants and their level of awareness regarding availability of men's range of the brands studied on consumers' purchase intentions of the brands stands rejected.**

7.0 Implications of the Study

The survey revealed certain interesting facts regarding the cosmetics brands under study. As far as general perception of consumers goes, L'Oreal has been mainly perceived as a premium brand that has created strong degree of differentiation in the market place. Fiama Di Wills by adopting the celebrity endorsement route [Deepika Padukone is the brand endorser (not for the men's range] and through the plots built within the advertisements has been perceived as a brand with an uninhibited appeal. Garnier has been perceived as a trusted brand that stands for effective grooming. Emami has been perceived as a cost-effective brand of cosmetics while Vaseline has been perceived as a trust worthy brand that delivers on what it promises. It was further observed that the customer perceptions regarding the brands were far more influenced by the advertisements in the mass media than their experiences of using the brands. It was observed that in the context of gender perception, L'Oreal and Fiama Di Wills were considered largely feminine while Garnier, Emami and Vaseline were considered neutral. Garnier, Emami and Vaseline have offered greater visibility to its men's range by advertising in the mass media; something that has not happened to a great extent as far as L'Oreal or Fiama Di Wills is concerned because of which consumer perception of femininity is strongly attached with those brands. That's exactly the reason why for brands like L'Oreal and Fiama Di Wills, majority of the informants have mentioned

'Not Aware' when they were queried regarding their awareness status of the men's range of the those brands while for the rest, most informants mentioned that they were 'Fully Aware'.

The brands that were considered for the study have for long catered to the requirements of women and it was largely felt that the men's range of the brands will not gain easy in roads into the male grooming market because they being considered 'gendered' brands. Promotion techniques related to the men's range need to be reconsidered. The men's range of the brands will be far more convincing to its target market if they are shown in situations that lend credibility and acceptance. One effective promotion route would be suitable product placements in movies and television.

One major aspect of the study was to find out if genders of respondents and their level of awareness regarding the men's range of the brands under study influenced the general perception, acceptance and purchase intention from the consumer's perspective. It was observed that the influence was significantly profound among men but negligible among women. Especially brand acceptability and purchase intention were the two aspects where significant variations in responses among the two categories of respondents were observed.

8.0 Limitations of the Study

- The study was largely conducted in the Kolkata market. A pan-Indian survey could have offered greater and more credible insights as far as the topic of study was concerned
- Few more 'gendered' brands from within the grooming market and also from other market verticals could have been included. That could have offered a more holistic view to the survey
- More variations in the context of respondent profile could have triggered some more interesting findings for the research study.

9.0 Conclusion

The men's grooming market in India is certainly a promising and lucrative segment for any marketer to get into but then large scale customization is required for the 'gendered' brands in terms of the composition of the brands, their packaging and promotion. Brands that have found success in promoting their products to women cannot continue to take the same route while targeting men. They need to rethink their promotional tools and techniques. They need to build on their strengths and add certain new rational and emotional elements to their communication mix that creates strong differentiation for the 'gendered' brands in the men's grooming segment. Brands that were considered for the survey enjoy high degrees of brand equity in the women's grooming market but then the key to seeking high brand equity in the men's grooming market will lie in relevant and calculated customization of the respective brand auras.

References:

- "Indian men take to fairness creams", available at http://daily.bhaskar.com/article/indian-men-take-to-fairness-creams-1434008.html, accessed May 29th 2011

- Grohmann Bianca (2009), "Gender Dimensions of Brand Personality", *Journal of Marketing Research*, Volume 46, Number 1, pp. 105-119
- Basu Indrajit (2006), "Indian men looking good", available at http://www.atimes.com/atimes/South_Asia/HA12Df03.html, accessed May 29th 2011
- Panda Tapan K.(2006), "Brand Gendering: A New Strategy for Building Brands", available at http://www.iupindia.in/1106/AE_Brand_Gendering_7.html, accessed May 29th 2011

- Alreck Pamela L.(1994), "Commentary: A New Formula for Gendering Products and Brands", *Journal of Product and Brand Management*, Volume 3, Number 1, pp. 6-18

Celebrity Endorsements & Sports Marketing

1.0 Introduction

Since the 1990s, it has been increasingly observed that sports personalities have occupied a significant chunk of the celebrity endorsement pie in the country. Professionals from the sporting arena are considered as role models by a large cross section of Indian youth and hence they are considered to be a potent force in the context of meaningfully selling brand attributes through endorsements. In the context of celebrity endorsements, movie stars have been found to claim the lion's share followed by sports celebrities. However, unlike movie stars, the popularity index of sports personalities experience frequent ups and downs based on their on-field performances.

One important aspect that has triggered the proliferation of sports celebrity endorsements in the country is the emergence of various sports management and celebrity management companies like Percept D'Mark, Nimbus, World Tel, 21st Century Management and Globosport. Over the years, these companies have reportedly spent millions in shaping the endorsement careers of various sporting personalities. The mushrooming of various sports management companies have ensured ample amount of brand endorsement scope to not just cricketers but also personalities involved with other sports. In the context of television advertising during the first decade of the 21st century, it has been found that while cricketers like Sachin Tendulkar, Sourav Ganguly, Rahul Dravid and MS Dhoni have endorsed a range of brands, there have sporting personalities like Leander Paes, Mahesh Bhupathi, Sania Mirza and Vishwanathan Anand who too have registered their presence when it comes to brand endorsements. Between January and

June 2011, an 11% jump in sports celebrity endorsement was reported as per TAM AdEx data compared to the same period in 2010 based on advertising volume – in seconds – during commercial time. Sports celebrities occupy 21% of the endorsement pie in the first half (H1) of 2011 compared to 10% in H1 2010 **(Exhibit-1.1)**.

Exhibit-1.1
Sports Celebrity Endorsement: Tracking a Quantum Leap

PROFESSION	SHARE % IN H1 2010	SHARE % IN H1 2011
Film Actress	45.29	38.53
Film Actor	41.86	36.95
Sports Person	10.45	20.88
TV Actor	1.34	1.96
TV Actress	1.06	1.68

TOP 10 ADVERTISERS (H1 2011)
1. HINDUSTAN UNILEVER
2. PROCTER & GAMBLE
3. PEPSICO
4. COLGATE PALMOLIVE INDIA
5. IDEA CELLULAR
6. GITANJALI GEMS
7. COCA COLA INDIA
8. PEPSICO INDIA HOLDINGS
9. RECKITT BENCKISER INDIA
10. L'OREAL INDIA

Source: http://www.hindustantimes.com

The TAM AdEx report of 2011 further revealed the top 10 sports celebrities based on ad volume in H1 2011 which mainly comprised of cricketers (past and present) **(Exhibit-1.2)**

Exhibit-1.2
The Top 10 Sports Celebrities

RANK	CELEBRITY
1	M S DHONI
2	SACHIN TENDULKAR
3	VIRAT KOHLI
4	VIRENDRA SEHWAG
5	YUVRAJ SINGH
6	IRFAN PATHAN
7	SAINA NEHWAL
8	AJIT AGARKAR
9	KAPIL DEV
10	ANIL KUMBLE

Source: Sharan Anita, "Celebrity ads add sports weight",
http://www.hindustantimes.com/Celebrity-ads-add-sports-weight/Article1-744442.aspx, September 11th

However one important trend that has been observed in the context of sports celebrity endorsements in the country is that cricketers have been far more successful in notching mega endorsement deals compared to celebrities from other sporting arenas. One important reason for this being that the level of interest and involvement among the general audience for cricket is huge and so is the fan following that most of the cricketers command. While on one hand, marketers are correct in estimating that cricketers can generate instant recognition and recall for a brand through endorsements, there is also an inherent risk involved. Cricketers are the cynosure of many and hence their on-field performances are closely observed. A lean patch or any sort of negativity associated with any cricketer has often been found to have a ripple effect on brands being endorsed by them. Also there are cricketers like Tendulkar and Dhoni who endorse multiple brands because of which there are various endorsements that do not get registered in the minds of audiences or they find difficulty in recalling brands.

Therefore it needs to be assessed that when it comes to sports celebrity endorsements, are cricketers the only viable option for companies. There needs to be a proper tool that can guide the marketers in selecting sports personalities who are able to establish a proper celebrity-brand image fit and are able to effectively connect with the target audiences of the brands being endorsed. The overall effectiveness of cricketers Vs sports personalities from other sporting domains needs to be analyzed in the context of sports celebrity endorsements.

2.0 Literature Review

Sports marketing as a term refers to the specific application of marketing principles and processes to sports products like teams, leagues, events etc and the marketing of non-sports products like FMCG, consumer durables etc. through associations with sports (Ghose, 2008). The entertainment aspect of sports along with the spread of mass media and increased leisure time has led to professionalism in sports. Increased popularity of various sports has produced myriads of sports fans that have prompted marketers to promote their products using the sports celebrity endorsement route.

While product brands need to maintain their quality, image and reputation in order to keep appealing to consumers, the yardstick for sports personality brands is their on-field performance that guarantees their recognition and popularity among the target audiences and sports management companies (Roy, 2007). The target audience for a majority of product categories comprise the youth and sports is definitely one aspect that appeals to a large cross section of them. Majority of marketers thus feel that sports personalities are highly effective in communicating brand ideas meaningfully.

Marketers have by and large completely ignored the fact that the popularity of various sports apart from cricket is increasing in this country. There have been a host of sports like soccer, tennis and hockey that have generated considerable and active participation among the youth. But then all that gets marketed in a big way are cricket related properties (Chatterjee, 2006). In other words there is a huge opportunity for marketers that are waiting to be tapped. There is opportunity for cost effective endorsements by establishing the right connect between brands and the target audience.

Sports convey a diverse range of emotion-laden values and symbols and it is the sports organizations that project these values and symbols through personalities and skills of their leading exponents (Farrelly, 2005). Sports sponsorships play an important role in a company's marketing mix and generate competitive advantage for a company if the resources are correctly identified and deployed in the marketplace.

Although extensive studies have been done in the context of the emergence of sports marketing in the country and the general science involved in managing celebrity endorsements, there has been lack of any in-depth research as far as the Indian sports celebrity endorsement scenario is concerned.

Marketers have been mostly found to stick with cricketers when it comes to brand endorsements and have not necessarily reaped rich rewards every time. Suitable techniques and insights need to be generated such that they act as a ready reckoner for marketers while zeroing on sports celebrities for brand endorsements.

3.0 Research Objectives

- To measure the familiarity of cricketers vis-à-vis other sports personalities under study
- To measure the popularity of cricketers vis-à-vis other sports personalities under study .
- To measure the Q-scores of cricketers vis-à-vis other sports personalities under study

- To understand the general audience perception of cricketers as brand endorsers
- To analyze the relative effectiveness of cricketers in establishing proper celebrity-brand image fit vis-à-vis other sports personalities
- To analyze the relative effectiveness of cricketers in connecting with the target audiences vis-à-vis other sports personalities

4.0 Research Hypotheses

H1: There is no significant difference between the genders of informants regarding their perception of cricketers as brand endorsers

H2: There is no significant difference between the genders of informants regarding their perception of cricketers establishing proper celebrity-brand image fit vis-à-vis other sports personalities

H3: There is no significant difference between the genders of informants regarding their perception of cricketers establishing suitable target audience connects vis-à-vis other sports personalities

5.0 Research Methodology

50 individuals in the age bracket of 25-45 years were surveyed. Majority of the respondents were service holders while the rest were students of the MBA program. Of the 50 individuals surveyed, 30 were male while 20 were female. Majority of the informants were post graduates with annual income between 2lacs and 3lacs. A combination of judgmental and convenience sampling was used to select the informants for the study. A structured questionnaire was used to collect responses. Responses were

sourced from the Kolkata market through personal interview method.

10 cricketers and 10 sports personalities representing other sporting arenas were shortlisted for the purpose of survey. **(Table-1.1)** highlights the sports celebrities shortlisted.

Table-1.1
Sports Personalities Shortlisted for Survey

Cricketers	Personalities from other Sports
MS Dhoni	Leander Paes
Rahul Dravid	Mahesh Bhupathi
Sachin Tendulkar	Sania Mirza
Virender Sehwag	Saina Nehwal
Harbhajan Singh	Abhinav Bindra
Yuvraj Singh	Vishwanathan Anand
Zaheer Khan	Narayan Karthikeyan
Gautam Gambhir	Vijender Singh
Virat Kohli	Bhaichung Bhutia
Suresh Raina	Jyoti Randhawa

6.0 Research Findings

The survey revealed certain interesting findings in the context of Q score measurement of the various sports celebrities under study. The Q score is a metric developed by Marketing Evaluations Inc. that measures the familiarity of a celebrity along with measuring the popularity a celebrity enjoys among the people familiar with the celebrity. The Q score measure of a celebrity (a sports celebrity in the present context) serves as a guide to marketers as far as selecting a celebrity for a brand endorsement is concerned.

The survey revealed that when it comes to cricketers, 100% of the informants were familiar with a cricketer but such was not the case when it comes to personalities representing sports other than cricket. The familiarity was less especially for those personalities who represent sports that do not enjoy high media exposure. To gain an insight regarding the popularity of the sports personalities under study, informants were asked to rate them. There were five options against each sports celebrity viz. **'One of my Favorite', 'Very Good', 'Good', 'Fair' and 'Poor'**. The popularity score is obtained based on the number of informants who rate a sports celebrity as **'One of my Favorite'**. **(Table-1.2)** highlights the familiarity and popularity score of all the sports celebrities under study.

Table-1.2
Sports Icons and their Respective Familiarity and Popularity Scores

Sportstar	Familiarity Score	Popularity Score
Sachin Tendulkar	50	32
Vishwanathan Anand	48	27
Bhaichung Bhutia	48	25
Virender Sehwag	50	23
Leander Paes	48	23
Rahul Dravid	50	21
MS Dhoni	50	19
Saina Nehwal	45	19
Yuvraj Singh	50	17
Narayan Karthikeyan	40	17
Sania Mirza	48	15
Vijender Singh	42	15
Mahesh Bhupathi	48	13
Harbhajan Singh	50	11
Gautam Gambhir	50	9
Zaheer Khan	50	7
Virat Kohli	50	7
Suresh Raina	50	7
Abhinav Bindra	42	7

The survey revealed that Sachin Tendulkar is one of the most attractive propositions for marketers when it comes to selecting sports celebrities for brand endorsements based on the Q score followed by Vishwanathan Anand and Bhaichung Bhutia. The survey further revealed that although all the cricketers shortlisted for the survey enjoyed

100% familiarity among the informants, there were only five cricketers who featured in the list of top 10 most appealing sports celebrities based on their Q scores **(Table-1.3)**.

Table-1.3
Q Scores of Top 10 Sports Celebrities under Study

Sportstar	Sports Associated With	Familiarity Score	Familiarity (%)	Popularity Score	Popularity (%)	"Q" Score
Sachin Tendulkar	Cricket	50	100	32	64	64
Vishwanathan Anand	Chess	48	96	27	54	54
Bhaichung Bhutia	Football	48	96	25	50	50
Virender Sehwag	Cricket	50	100	23	46	46
Leander Paes	Tennis	48	96	23	46	46
Rahul Dravid	Cricket	50	100	21	42	42
MS Dhoni	Cricket	50	100	19	38	38
Saina Nehwal	Badminton	45	90	19	38	38
Yuvraj Singh	Cricket	50	100	17	34	34
Narayan Karthikeyan	F1 Car Racing	40	80	17	34	34

Informants of the survey were asked if they perceived cricketers to be over rated as brand endorsers. They were given five options to clarify their view point viz. **'Absolutely Agree', 'Agree to a certain extent', 'Neutral', 'Disagree to a certain extent'** and **'Absolutely Disagree'**. 40% of the male respondents absolutely agreed that cricketers are over rated, 33.3% of the male respondents agreed to a certain extent while the rest were either neutral or disagreed to a certain extent. 40% of the female respondents absolutely agreed while almost the same percentage of female respondents agreed to a certain extent. Overall, 40% of the respondents absolutely agreed that cricketers were over rated as brand endorsers.

The need was felt to find out if any significant differences between the genders of informants regarding their perception of cricketers as brand endorsers existed for which a Chi –square test was employed. For testing H1, the calculated value of chi-square was found to be 5.94. The table value of chi-square at 95% level of confidence and at d.f=4 is 9.49. **Since table value of χ^2 (9.49) > calculated value of χ^2 (5.94), H1 which states that there is no significant difference between the genders of informants regarding their perception of cricketers as brand endorsers stands accepted.**

Informants of the survey were asked if sports celebrities from sporting arenas other than cricket were as good as cricketers when as far as establishing a proper celebrity-brand image fit in the context of endorsements was concerned. 40% of the male respondents and 50% of the female respondents absolutely subscribed to the viewpoint that non-cricketing sports celebrities were equally effective in establishing suitable celebrity-brand image fit. For testing H2, a chi-square test was employed. The calculated value of chi-square was found to be 0.28. The table value of chi-square at 95% level of confidence and at d.f=4 is 9.49. **Since table value of χ^2 (9.49) > calculated value of χ^2 (0.28), H2 which states that there is no significant difference between the genders of informants regarding their perception of cricketers establishing proper celebrity-brand image fit vis-à-vis other sports personalities stands accepted.**

Informants of the survey were asked to observe their viewpoint regarding the following statement - 'Its only cricketers who can actually connect with the target audience of the brands being endorsed in the context of sports celebrity endorsements'. Majority of the male (30%) and female (35%) respondents agreed to a certain extent as far as the statement was concerned. For testing H3, a chi-square test was employed. The calculated value of chi-square was found to be 0.79. The table value of chi-square at 95% level of confidence and at d.f=4 is 9.49. **Since table value of χ^2 (9.49) > calculated value of χ^2 (0.79), H3 which states that there is no significant difference between the genders of informants regarding their perception of cricketers establishing suitable target audience connects vis-à-vis other sports personalities stands accepted.**

7.0 Implications of the Study

The survey offered certain interesting insights regarding audience perception of sports celebrities in the context of brand endorsements. Familiarity and popularity are the determinants of a celebrity's Q score. The survey revealed that although 100% of the informants were familiar with the cricketers when it came to rating them as one of their favorites, only five cricketers featured in the top 10. Another interesting observation was that all sports celebrities who featured in the top 10 based on their Q scores were personalities who have been representing the country for sufficiently long time in the international circuit. In other words, a sports celebrity seeks popularity through the achievements obtained in one's sporting arena over a significant period of time. The survey revealed that Sachin Tendulkar was way ahead of his contemporaries in cricketing and non-cricketing arena in terms of Q score. He is the most attractive proposition for marketers when it comes to endorsing brands.

Cricketers have mostly been the cynosure of marketers when it comes to sports celebrity endorsements in the country but then this strategy has not always been a lucrative proposition for them. The survey indicated the general perception of people in the context of sports celebrity endorsements. Informants by and large were found to share the view point that cricketers were over rated as brand endorsers. Moreover they felt that non-cricketing sports celebrities were as effective as their cricketing counterparts in terms of establishing proper celebrity-brand image fit. However they were found to agree to a certain extent that the cricketers are more effective in connecting with the target audience of brands compared to their counterparts in other sporting arenas.

8.0 Limitations of the Study

- The study was conducted in the Kolkata market. A pan-Indian survey

could have offered a more holistic insight into the topic of study
- Sports celebrities considered for the survey were based on the judgment of the author. Alterations in the list of celebrities might have yielded a different conclusion to the study
- More variations in the context of informant profile could have generated some more insightful findings for the research study.

9.0 Conclusion

Marketers have long been found to invest in cricketers when it comes to selecting endorsers for brand promotions. The simple idea behind the strategy is that the game of cricket and its players command the maximum media exposure and eyeballs in the country. However this idea has not always been found to work in favor of marketers' investments. It has been revealed through the survey that sports personalities from arenas other than cricket are almost an equally viable alternative in the context of sports celebrity endorsements. Marketers need to go by certain appropriate tools and techniques while selecting sports celebrities and should also acknowledge the dominant perception of the sports audiences in the country in the said context.

References:

- *Sharan Anita (2011), "Celebrity ads add sports weight", http://www.hindustantimes.com/Celebrity-ads-add-sports-weight/Article1-744442.aspx.*

- *Ghose Amitabha (2008), "Dynamics of Sports Marketing", The Icfai University Press, First Edition, pp. 3-11*

- Roy Kisholoy (2007), "Sports Celebrity Endorsement in India: Cricket and the Sourav Ganguly Saga", http://www.iupindia.in/807/MM_Sports_Celebrity_Endorsement_in_India_58.html
- Chatterjee Purvita (2006), "Business of Sports", http://www.thehindubusinessline.in/catalyst/2006/10/05/stories/2006100500060100.htm
- Farrelly Francis (2005), "Sports Sponsorship Linked Marketing and Public Relations: An Investigation of Key Resources and Capabilities", http://www.austlii.edu.au/au/journals/MonashBusRw/2005/20.html

Celebrity Endorsements and Men's Intimate Wear

1.0 Introduction

Celebrities are popular among the public and they take pleasure in being recognized by numerous people. Good looks, classy life styles and special skills are only some of celebrity's special features that are different general people and are seen by the public, which grants them a large amount of the public's attention. It explains that a celebrity is a person such as an actor, sportsman, entertainer etc who is different from the general public and is recognized by them because of his or her achievements. One of the methods that firms use for their brand communication is celebrity endorsement. In this method they use celebrities to play the role of the spokes person for their brand, which assures their brand's place within the society by promoting the celebrity's personality, fame and their influence on the public's decision. Celebrity endorsement can play vital leading role when it comes to influencing the public's decision in a market which has vast no. of local, regional and international brands. In recent years using celebrity endorsements for brand promotions has gathered phenomenal momentum.

The present study involves analyzing the effects of celebrity endorsements on men's innerwear brands. Men's innerwear is divided into three sub categories viz. vest, briefs and thermals. For quite some years now, it has been observed that leading national brands of innerwear like Rupa Frontline, Luz Cozi, Dollar Bigboss and Amul Macho have adopted celebrity endorsements to promote themselves. Leading movie stars of the country like Sunny Deol, Shah Rukh Khan, Akshay Kumar, Salman Khan and Saif Ali Khan have been found to endorse various brands of men's innerwear. As per various brand communication experts, there has been a shift in the thought process of customers when it comes to buying men's innerwear. Apart from comfort, styling and design have gained equal prominence and with a plethora of brand options available, marketers have identified celebrity endorsements as an effective tool to promote men's innerwear brands.

2.0 Literature Study

Celebrity endorsement is way of communicating the idea of any product from the manufacturers end to the customer by using the image of a personality or an endorser (Agarwal and Dubey, 2012). People generally tend to buy those products which their favorite personalities have endorsed. Successful branding programs are initiated for the same purpose. The message that the company tries to convey through this programs is that there is no other product like their product in the market, in a way they show that customers have just their product as the best option and thus compels the customers to buy that particular product.

In today's world companies are investing more and more on celebrities to promote their brand (Sonwalkar et al., 2011). The use of celebrities is increasing and so is the case of the impact that it creates on the minds of the consumers. In many cases it can be seen that liking for a certain product can be created through endorsements. Endorsements often enhance the recall for brands.

The use of integrated marketing communication has played a huge role in bringing the desired message required for targeting the mass (Patra and Datta, 2010). The emergence of celebrity endorsement in India started with the advent of globalization, the need for celebrities who are accepted among the masses created a buzz for different products. The use of suitable celebrity for a particular brand and product type is a concern for all companies. The emerging trend and challenges have compelled companies to think of the endorsers whether it is a sports personality or a movie star who will be accepted by the people for a particular product category.

Celebrity endorsements can have negative results (Patel, 2009) and may boomerang if not utilized properly by the company. This is because even celebrities have human short comings and can fail in their field or get involved in controversies this can in turn have negative impact on the product they endorse which might fail in spite of being competitive quality.

Celebrity endorsements for products have a positive impact on the consumer buying behavior. With the implementation of adaptive conjoint analysis and genetic algorithms in the advertising process, advertisers have newly approached the matching of product and celebrity attributes (Zwilling and Fruchter, 2013).

The present study aims at evaluating the effects of endorsements on men's innerwear brands and also the endorsements effects on consumer purchase behavior of the above mentioned product category.

3.0 Research Methodology

The study was conducted in Kolkata among 50 respondents (29 males and 21 females) mainly belonging to the 21 to 40 age bracket using convenient sampling technique. The communication content for men's innerwear brand was considered as the independent variable while the effects of celebrity endorsements on brands and consumer purchase behavior were considered as the dependent variable for the survey.

4.0 Research Objectives

- To analyze the effect of celebrity endorsements on men's innerwear brands advertised.
- To analyzethe consumer purchase behavior of men's innerwear brands advertised.

5.0 Research Hypotheses

The following hypotheses were developed for the purpose of the study:

$H1_0$: Effects of celebrity endorsements of men's innerwear brands have been perceived similarly across genders of respondents

$H2_0$: Consumer purchase behavior of men's innerwear brands is significantly different across genders of respondents

6.0 Research Findings

This section deals with analyzing the responses gathered from the informants of the study and also tests the two hypotheses developed for the study using statistical tool (SPSS – Version 19).

6.1 Descriptive Statistics

Respondents of the study were asked to express their opinion regarding the effects of celebrity endorsement on men's innerwear brand and also on their purchase behavior related to men's innerwear brand. Majority of the respondents (62%) were found to agree that celebrity endorsements of men's innerwear brand enhance brand awareness. 38% of the respondents stated that celebrity endorsements influenced the brand loyalty for men's innerwear brands in a positive way. 46% of the respondents opined that celebrity endorsements enhanced perceived quality of brand and brand association among men's innerwear brands. 54% of the respondents stated that celebrity endorsements of men's innerwear brand enhanced brand recall.

Majority of the respondents (62%) mentioned that they did have specific brand choice in their minds when they went to purchase innerwear at retail outlets. However when the respondents were asked that whether the brand choice was shaped by the advertisements that they saw in the media only 50% agreed to this view point. It was further observed that 61% of the respondents opined that they did not buy a particular brand because their favorite celebrity was endorsing it.62% of the respondents have also disagreed to the view point that they wish to be like their favorite celebrity when they buy a particular brand of innerwear.

Exhibit 1.1 presents the perceived effects of endorsements and the percentage of responses that mentioned the enhancement of the effects due to endorsements in a graphical format.

Exhibit 1.1: Perceived Effects of Endorsements by Respondents

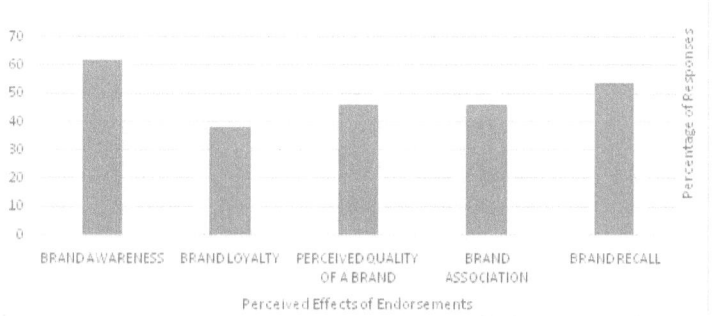

6.2 Testing Of Hypotheses

Two null hypotheses were developed for the purpose of study.

$H1_0$: Effects of celebrity endorsements of men's innerwear brand have been perceived similarly across genders of respondents

To test the first null hypothesis an independent sample t test was adopted to measure the perceived effect of endorsement across genders of respondents. The mean scores of the genders of respondents were found to be 3.41 for males and 3.66 for females. Thus suggesting the absence of significant difference between the mean scores of the gender profiles considered for the study. The p-value of the independent sample t test was found to be 0.446. Since the p-value obtained is greater than 0.05 (p>0.05), the null hypothesis viz. **Effects of celebrity endorsements of men's innerwear brand have been perceived similarly across genders of respondents** stands accepted.

Table 1.1: Independent Sample t test to Measure Perceived Effects of Endorsements across Genders of Respondents

Variable		Mean	Std. dev.	t-value	p-value
Gender	Male	3.41	1.037	-0.768	0.446
	Female	3.66	1.168		

$H2_0$: *Consumer purchase behavior of men's innerwear brands is significantly different across genders of respondents*

To test the second null hypothesis an independent sample t test was adopted to measure the customer purchase behavior across genders of respondents. The mean scores of the genders of respondents were found to be 1.97 for males and 3.11 for females. Thus suggesting that significant difference between the mean scores of the gender profiles existed. The p-value of the independent sample t test was found to be 0.001. Since the p-value obtained is less than 0.05 ($p<0.05$), the null hypothesis stands rejected and the alternate hypothesis ($H1_a$) viz. **Consumer purchase behavior of men's innerwear brands is not significantly different across genders ofrespondents** stands accepted.

Table 1.2: Independent Sample t test to Measure Consumer Purchase Behavior across Genders of Respondents

Variable		Mean	Std. dev.	t-value	p-value
Gender	Male	1.97	0.848	-3.872	0.001
	Female	3.11	1.203		

7.0 Implications of the Study

The study revealed certain interesting insights on the perceived effects of endorsements on brands by the respondents and also the effects of endorsements on the customer purchase behavior as far as men's innerwear brands were concerned.

While majority of the respondents did believe that celebrity endorsements enhanced brand awareness, brand association and brand recall to a great extent, they however did not subscribe to the idea that endorsements contributed to enhanced brand loyalty.

Also informants for the study did mention that they had certain brands in their minds when they go to shop for men's innerwear but then not much of this is attributable to the advertisements seen in the media and definitely not attributable to endorsements. Respondents have no desire as such to adopt a brand just because their favorite celebrity endorses it or to feel like the celebrity or an extension of the celebrity.

No differences as such between male and female respondents considered for the study was found as far as perceived effects of brand endorsements were concerned and also no significant differences were reported in the customer purchase behavior among males and females in the context of men's innerwear.

8.0 Limitations of the Study

- The study was conducted in Kolkata market only. A pan-India study could have of better insight into the topic of study
- More variations in the profile of informants could have generated some more insightful findings
- The sample size was relatively small from which primary data has been collected. Hence the conclusion drawn are area specific and any generalization will need a cautious approach

9.0 References

- Agrawal, Pradeep and Dubey, S.K. (2012), "Celebrities: The Linking Pin between Brands & Their Customer", *International Journal of Management & Business Studies*, 2(1), 56-60

- Patel, Pratik C. (2009), "Impact of Celebrity Endorsement on Brand Acceptance", The Icfai University Journal of Consumer Behavior, IV(1), 36-45

- Patra, Supriyo and Datta, Saroj K. (2010), "Celebrity Endorsement in India- Emerging Trends and Challenges", 5(3), 16-23

- Sonwalkar, Jayant, Kapse, Manohar and Pathak, Anuradha (2011), "Celebrity Impact – A Model of Celebrity Endorsement", *Journal of*

Marketing & Communication, 7(1), 34-40

- Zwilling, Moti and Fruchter, Gila E. (2013), "Matching Product Attributes to Celebrities who Reinforce the Brand: An Innovative Algorithmic Selection Model", *Journal of Advertising Research*, 53(4), 391-410

Celebrity Endorsements & Industrial Products

1.0 Introduction

The construction sector is a significant contributor in the economy of any country. India is no exception as this sector has been found to be a major employment driver and with the current focus on developing the country's infrastructure this sector looks to be a promising proposition.

With the positive future forecast for the construction business and intensified competition, players in the sector have been found to continuously strategize to retain and expand their market share. The otherwise generic products related to this industry like cement, steel rods, TMT bars paints, plywood etc are being consciously given a brand identity so that strong differentiation can be established.

Apart from highlighting the key strengths or characteristics of the products, the focus of communication has often been on the parent company and its inherent strengths. Companies like Tata, Birla, J.K., L&T have often been found to adopt this kind of communication endeavors but then apart from this mode of communication, many of the them and the other players in the industry have lately been found to pursue celebrities to endorse their products. There is a strong belief among the marketers of construction products brands that by associating with celebrities, their products will be getting an additional advantage and will be able to leverage on the positive traits of the celebrities.

Across the nation, when it comes to endorsing construction product brands, it has been observed that both national and local celebrities have endorsed such products. We find Amitabh Bachchan endorsing Binani cement, Sourav Ganguly, Mithun Chakraborty endorsing various brands of TMT bars and Shah Rukh Khan endorsing Concast Maxx steel rods. Such advertisements have been observed in TVCs, in the print media and also in the outdoor media. Celebrity endorsements at the end of the day are believed to enhance the awareness for construction product brands and also impact the various elements of brand equity in a positive way.

For the purpose of this study, the researchers have considered three different products associated with the construction business viz. cement, TMT bars and steel bars.

2.0 Literature Review

Endorsement is a means of communication where celebrities (individuals known to the public for their achievements) act as spokesperson of the brand and by extending their popularity and personality they certify the brand's claim and position. The basic assumption underlying celebrity endorsement is that the value associated with the celebrity is transferred to the brand and therefore it helps in creating an image that can be easily referred by consumers. With the advent of mass media a great amount of interest has been taken in the area of celebrity endorsements and the impact they create which has seen corporates investing in celebrities to promote their products. (Sonwalkar et al, 2011).

The increase in importance of endorsements has offered new challenges for marketers (Patra & Datta, 2010). There have been various studies undertaken to identify the various strengths and weaknesses associated with the celebrity endorsements and techniques and models have been developed to overcome the challenges associated while selecting celebrities as brand endorsers in the Indian context. It has been found that Indian celebrities often endorse multiple brands and their familiarity and popularity played an important role as far as their effectiveness as endorsers are concerned.

The celebrity endorsing the product has to have an image which is in sync with the image and, attributes of the brand being endorsed and such endorsements need to have a positive impact on the target audiences for the brand being endorsed (Marshall et al, 2008). Incongruity between image of the endorser and the brand image often leads to post purchase dissonance which many a times lead to customer dissatisfaction later on.

Multiplicity of endorsements has led to clutter and confusion among the target audiences of various brands which has often been found to negatively impact the recall of brands (Khatri, 2006). Until and unless an endorsement is backed by a strong and differentiating idea, it is difficult for an endorsement to grab the attention of customers. There are several risks associated with endorsements which need to be carefully considered by marketers. Studies using models and concepts like source credibility, match up hypothesis, model of meaning transfer and multi product endorsement has contributed to drawing relationships between celebrities, the brands they endorse and the perception of the target audiences. These studies indicate that the likeability, personality, credibility of the celebrity is an influencing factor which impact endorsements.

Celebrity endorsements have often been found to play a significant role when it comes to endorsing products in the B2B market (Canning & Douglas, 2006). The meaning portrayed through the celebrities' image with that of the product affects the behavior derived from the customers. The other factors like credibility, reliability, trustworthiness, expertise, attractiveness, dependability of the celebrity also makes a significant difference to the perceptions of the customers in the B2B industry. The importance of specialized marketing communications like celebrity endorsement in the B2B markets thus cannot be ignored.

Consumers are different from each other in multiple ways and so does their perceptions (Biswas et al, 2006). Celebrities who are believed to have the expertise to endorse certain products are found to be more acceptable as endorsers of those products. Subsequently the amount of brand acceptability also gets enhanced in such cases. Further expert endorsers have been found to play a bigger role in generating positive brand perceptions than celebrities when it comes to technology oriented products. The perceived congruency between the endorser and the product can play an influential role in neutralizing potentially stronger effects of expert endorsements in some instances.

The present study deals with analyzing the impact of genders and age profiles of respondents on various elements of brand equity as far as construction product brands are concerned.

3.0 Research objectives

- To study the role of celebrity endorsements in generating brand awareness for construction product brands
- To analyze the contribution of the celebrity endorsement to the perceived quality of construction product brands

- To understand the role of celebrity endorsements in facilitating brand associations of construction product brands
- To analyze the contribution of celebrity endorsements to the brand loyalty for construction product brands

4.0 Research Hypothesis

H1 (i): There are no significant differences between the genders of respondents on their awareness of construction product brands generated through celebrity endorsements.

H1 (ii): There are no significant differences between the age profiles of the respondents on their awareness of construction product brands generated through celebrity endorsements.

H1 (iii): There is no significant interaction between the genders and age profiles of respondents on their awareness of construction product brands generated through celebrity endorsements.

H2 (i): There are no significant differences between the genders of respondents on their perceived quality of construction product brands generated through celebrity endorsements.

H2 (ii): There are no significant differences between the age profiles of the respondents on their perceived quality of construction product brands generated through celebrity endorsements.

H2 (iii): There is no significant interaction between the genders and age profiles of respondents on their perceived quality of construction product brands generated through celebrity endorsements.

H3 (i): There are no significant differences between the genders of respondents on their brand association of construction product brands generated through celebrity endorsements.

H3 (ii): There are no significant differences between the age profiles of the respondents on their brand association of construction product brands generated through celebrity endorsements.

H3 (iii): There is no significant interaction between the genders and age profiles of respondents on their brand association of construction product brands generated through celebrity endorsements.

H4 (i): There are no significant differences between the genders of respondents on their brand loyalty of construction product brands generated through celebrity endorsements.

H4 (ii): There are no significant differences between the age profiles of the respondents on their brand loyalty of construction product brands generated through celebrity endorsements.

H4 (iii): There is no significant interaction between the genders and age profiles of respondents on their brand loyalty of construction product brands generated through celebrity endorsements.

5.0 Research Methodology

60 individuals in the age bracket of 21 to 40 years were surveyed. The informants considered for the survey were graduates/post graduates; some were

students, service holders and self-employed. All the informants considered for the survey were based in Kolkata. A combination of convenience and judgmental sampling technique was used for the survey. Of the 60 individuals surveyed 40 were males and 20 were females. A structured questionnaire was used to collect the responses.

Responses were sourced through personal interview method. The statistical method used to evaluate the observations of the study was **two-way ANOVA** for which three separate hypotheses were developed for each aspect of study to study the impact of independent variables individually and also to study their interaction on a particular aspect of study.

6.0 Research Findings

The informants of the survey were asked to make observations on various elements of brand equity namely **brand awareness, perceived quality, brand association** and **brand loyalty** as far as construction product brands are concerned.

In order to understand the effects of age, gender and the interaction of age and gender on the brand awareness of construction product brands a two-way ANOVA was employed as a suitable statistical test for the exercise. The two-way ANOVA offered three separate p-values for gender (p=0.629), age (p=0.669) and the interaction of gender and age (p=0.389) **(Table 1)**. Since all the three p-values obtained are more than 0.05 (p>0.05); **H1 (i) which states that there are no significant differences between the genders of respondents on their awareness of construction product brands generated through celebrity endorsements stands accepted.**

H1 (ii) **which states that there are no significant differences between the age profiles of the respondents on their awareness of construction product brands generated through celebrity endorsements stands accepted.**

H1 (iii) **which states that there is no significant interaction between the genders and age profiles of respondents on their awareness of construction** product brands generated through celebrity endorsements stands accepted.

Table 1

Dependent Variable: BRAND AWARENESS

Source	Type III Sum of Squares	Df	Mean Square	F	Sig.
Corrected Model	4.121^a	7	.589	.885	.525
Intercept	582.456	1	582.456	875.579	.000
GENDER	.157	1	.157	.236	.629
AGE	1.043	3	.348	.522	.669
GENDER * AGE	2.044	3	.681	1.024	.389
Error	34.592	52	.665		
Total	893.750	60			
Corrected Total	38.712	59			

a. R Squared = .106 (Adjusted R Squared = -.014)

In order to understand the effects of age, gender and the interaction of age and gender on the perceived quality of construction product brands a two-way ANOVA was employed as a suitable statistical test for the exercise. The 2-way ANOVA offered three separate p-values for gender (p=0.433), age (p=0.633) and the interaction of gender and age (p=0.835) **(Table 2).** Since all the three p-values obtained are more than 0.05 (p>0.05); **H2 (i) which states that there are no significant differences between the genders of respondents on their perceived quality of construction product brands generated through celebrity endorsements stands accepted.**

H2 (ii): There are no significant differences between the age profiles of the respondents on their perceived quality of construction product brands generated through celebrity endorsements stands accepted.

H2 (iii): There is no significant interaction between the genders and age profiles of respondents on their perceived quality of construction product brands generated through celebrity endorsements stands accepted.

Table 2

Dependent Variable: PERCEIVED QUALITY

Source	Type III Sum of Squares	Df	Mean Square	F	Sig.
Corrected Model	2.355a	7	.336	.343	.930
Intercept	256.241	1	256.241	261.037	.000
GENDER	.612	1	.612	.624	.433
AGE	1.699	3	.566	.577	.633
GENDER * AGE	.845	3	.282	.287	.835
Error	51.045	52	.982		
Total	459.000	60			
Corrected Total	53.400	59			

a. R Squared = .044 (Adjusted R Squared = -.085)

In order to understand the effects of age, gender and the interaction of age and gender on the brand association of construction product brands a two-way ANOVA was employed as a suitable statistical test for the exercise. The 2-way ANOVA offered three separate p-values for gender (p=0.538), age (p=0.654) and the interaction of gender and age (p=0.774) (Table 3). Since all the three p-values obtained are more than 0.05 (p>0.05); H3 (i) which states that there are no significant differences between the genders of respondents on their brand association of construction product brands generated through celebrity endorsements stands accepted

H3 (ii) which states that there are no significant differences between the age profiles of the respondents on their brand association of construction product brands generated through celebrity endorsements stands accepted

H3 (iii) which states that there is no significant interaction between the genders and age profiles of respondents on their brand association of construction product brands generated through celebrity endorsements stands accepted.

Table 3

Dependent Variable: BRAND ASSOCIATION

Source	Type III Sum of Squares	Df	Mean Square	F	Sig.
Corrected Model	2.100[a]	7	.300	.404	.896
Intercept	288.428	1	288.428	388.223	.000
GENDER	.286	1	.286	.385	.538
AGE	1.214	3	.405	.545	.654
GENDER * AGE	.829	3	.276	.372	.774
Error	38.633	52	.743		
Total	489.000	60			
Corrected Total	40.733	59			

a. R Squared = .052 (Adjusted R Squared = -.076)

In order to understand the effects of age, gender and the interaction of age and gender on the brand loyalty of construction product brands a two-way ANOVA was employed as a suitable statistical test for the exercise. The 2-Way ANOVA offered three separate p-values for gender (p=0.268), age (p=0.956) and the interaction of gender and age (p=0.253) (Table 4). Since all the three p-values obtained are more than 0.05 (p>0.05); **H4 (i)** which states that there are no significant differences between the genders of respondents on their brand loyalty of construction product brands generated through celebrity endorsements stands accepted.

H4 (ii) which states that there are no significant differences between the age profiles of the respondents on their brand loyalty of construction product brands generated through celebrity endorsements stands accepted.

H4 (iii) which states that there is no significant interaction between the genders and age profiles of respondents on their brand loyalty of construction product brands generated through celebrity endorsements stands accepted.

Table 4

Dependent Variable: BRAND LOYALTY

Source	Type III Sum of Squares	Df	Mean Square	F	Sig.
Corrected Model	2.286a	7	.327	.803	.589
Intercept	278.489	1	278.489	684.474	.000
GENDER	.509	1	.509	1.252	.268
AGE	.130	3	.043	.106	.956
GENDER * AGE	1.709	3	.570	1.400	.253
Error	21.157	52	.407		
Total	430.778	60			
Corrected Total	23.443	59			

a. R Squared = .097 (Adjusted R Squared = -.024)

7.0 Implications of the Study

The survey revealed certain interesting insights as far as the effects of celebrity endorsements on various elements of brand equity in the context of construction product brands are concerned. The two-way ANOVA employed for hypotheses testing revealed that there was no statistical significance as far as the impact of genders of respondents, impact of age profiles of respondents and the interaction of the two above mentioned independent variables on various elements of brand equity are concerned. The study revealed that informants for the survey largely believed that celebrities did impact their purchase decisions in case of construction product brands and the celebrities had a greater impact on the target audiences than intermediary and word of mouth (offered by friends, family members and peers) recommendations.

8.0 Limitations of the Study

- The study was conducted in Kolkata only. A pan-India based study could have offered a more holistic idea of the subject
- The study was confined to just three products related to the construction business viz. cement, TMT bars and steel bars. Involving few other products from the industry could have offered a more wholesome learning

- More variations in the professional profiles of respondents could have offered some more interesting observations regarding the impact of endorsements on various elements of brand equity.

9.0 Conclusion

Over the years, marketers across the industry verticals have endorsed the view point that celebrities play a major role as far as reaching out to the target audiences of a brand is concerned. Although there are certain challenges and caveats involved with the execution of celebrity endorsements, if planned and executed properly, it has been observed to pay rich dividends to companies. The present study which was undertaken to analyze the impact of endorsements on various elements of brand equity in the context of construction product brands revealed similarly that celebrities do play an equally important role in enhancing the appeal of industrial products just as they do for FMCGs, consumer durables and other product categories.

References

- Sonwalkar Jayant, Kapse Manohar and Pathak Anuradha (2011), "Celebrity Impact – A Model of Celebrity Endorsement", *Journal of Marketing & Communication*, 7(1), pp 34-40
- Patra Supriyo and Datta Saroj K. (2010), "Celebrity Endorsement in India- Emerging Trends and Challenges", 5(3), pp 16-23
- Marshall Roger, NA Woonbong, State Gabriel and Deuskar Sonali (2008), "Endorsement Theory: How Consumers Relate to Celebrity Models", *Journal of Advertising Research*, 48(4), pp 564-572
- Khatri Puja (2006), "Celebrity Endorsement: A Strategic Promotion Perspective", *Indian Media Studies Journal*, 1(1), pp 25-37
- Biswas Dipayan, Biswas Abhijit and Das Neel (2006), "The Differential Effects of Celebrity and Expert Endorsements On Consumer Risk

Perceptions", *Journal of Advertising*, 35(2), pp 17-31

- Canning Louise E and West Douglas (2006), "Celebrity endorsement in business markets", *www.impgroup.org/uploads/papers/5651.pdf*

Celebrity Endorser Types & Product Categories

1.0 Introduction

In the present age of marketing communication, it has often been noticed that audiences and readers consciously try to evade advertisements while flipping through newspapers or magazines or while they are listening to radio or watching television. It is due to this reason that many marketers have adopted the strategy of celebrity endorsements for brands which is a form of differentiated communication and is of great significance for brands being advertised. Celebrity endorsements have facilitated the activity of marketers to capture the perceptual territory of potential customers and it is further found that celebrities often catalyze brand acceptance and offer momentum to brands by endorsing their intrinsic value.

Celebrities often refer to those personalities who enjoy significantly higher amount of public adulation compared to the common people. They are generally known for their achievements in a domain that is distinctly different from that of the product class endorsed (Agrawal & Dubey, 2012). Two reasons why advertisers need endorsements are to increase credibility and attractiveness of their advertisements which influences the attitude of customers towards brands. There is a well-defined push and pull mechanism that is in operation when it comes to endorsements as on one hand, celebrities are found to push brands aggressively and on the other hand pull a few millions in their kitty. Celebrities are supposed to create a positive rub-off effect on products and it is mainly the popularity and appeal of the celebrities that enables the rub off effect to be executed in a positive way.

The present study focuses on the effective contributions made by various celebrity endorser types across endorsements of various product categories considered for the study viz. FMCG, consumer durables, pharmaceutical products and financial service products. The parameters selected to classify celebrity types for the purpose of study are the celebrity's professional life cycle (emerging vs. matured celebrity), controversial nature of celebrity (controversial vs. non controversial celebrity), country of origin of celebrity (Indian vs foreign celebrity), multiple brand endorsements by celebrity (multiple brand endorser vs. single brand endorser) and nature of appearance of celebrity in a commercial (real vs. fictional appearance of a celebrity in a commercial). FMCG, consumer durables, pharmaceutical products and financial service products.

2.0 Literature Review

Efforts have been made to investigate the interactive impact of endorser and product characteristics on advertising effectiveness (Lee & Thorson, 2008). The persuasiveness of endorsements differs with the degree of celebrity-product congruence. It is further felt that consumers are more likely to be impacted by the celebrity-product congruence when they are motivated to elaborate on an advertisement.

A foreign celebrity or foreign brand name can enhance or may prove detrimental for a brand in terms of consumer attitude, product quality perception and purchase intention in another country (Chao et al, 2005). When firms expand globally, they are faced with certain important decision making in the areas of production locations, entry modes and advertising and promotions. In addition to the country of origin effects that can have a positive or negative repercussion for a brand, there is the issue of whether a foreign celebrity can moderate the country of origin effects for a brand.

There are certain factors that influence effectiveness of celebrity endorsements and there are factors that predict the effectiveness of an endorsement exercise. It has been observed that celebrities who endorse a range of products are perceived by consumers as less credible compared to those celebrities who endorse one brand (Silvera & Austad, 2004). Further there is always a doubt in the minds of consumers regarding whether a celebrity has true liking for the product he/she is endorsing.

There are some of the key predictors of celebrity endorsements viz. celebrity performance, negative information, celebrity credibility, celebrity expertise, celebrity trustworthiness, celebrity attractiveness, celebrity familiarity, celebrity likeability and celebrity-product fit (Amos et al, 2008). Among the predictors, it was observed that negative celebrity information had the most influence on advertising effectiveness followed by celebrity trustworthiness and then celebrity expertise.

It is widely felt that celebrities known from movies and television can give endorsements *in character* (which basically relates to celebrities playing fictional roles both in movies or on television and in commercials). The image of the celebrity does not influence the brand image of the product that is being advertised but it is the image of the character that the celebrity plays (Spilski & Klein, 2008). It needs to be analyzed if the appropriate media context-that creates the stage persona of the endorser be compared with an inappropriate media context for an in-character endorsement.

In the present era, advertisements play a significant role in changing customer perceptions towards a product. Studies have been undertaken to understand consumer perception of celebrity versus non celebrity advertisements on television as far as fast moving consumer goods are concerned (Parmar & Patel, 2014). Significant difference for all FMCG categories between advertisements for celebrity and non-celebrity has been observed. Studies have also indicated that advertisements featuring celebrities have bestowed special attributes upon a consumer durable product that it may have lacked otherwise (Rai, 2013).

The factors that determine the appropriateness of a celebrity to endorse a product is not quite clear (Choi & Rifon,

2012). A cognitive approach that focuses on consumers' attributions of celebrity endorsement motives has been used to understand the "match-up" effects in celebrity endorsements. The process of consumer attributions of a celebrity's motive and the subsequent effects of these attributions on the consumer evaluations of the endorser, the ad and the brand involved in the endorsement have also been studied.

Celebrity endorsement as a persuasive communication strategy is not just restricted to FMCGs and consumer durables but also to direct-to-consumer pharmaceuticals (Kim & Park, 2011). A theoretical framework has been developed in the said context that predicts the independent and interactive effects of celebrity-product congruence and attribution of celebrity endorsement motive. Greater effects of celebrity-product congruence have been observed when motive of celebrity endorsement was internally attributed.

While there are number of studies that have concentrated on the interactive effects of celebrities and products in general, specific influences between a particular celebrity type on different product categories has not been studied; especially so in the Indian context. It is necessary to appreciate whether similar influences are observed across product categories in the context of a particular celebrity type.

3.0 Research Methodology

The major objective of the research study is to observe the nature of influence exerted by a particular celebrity type on the product categories considered for the survey viz. FMCG, consumer durable, pharmaceutical products and financial service products.

150 individuals (male and female) in the age bracket of 21-50 years were surveyed in the city of Kolkata for the purpose of study. Majority of the respondents were students followed by service holders, business people and few were homemakers. A structured questionnaire comprising 20 questions constructed on five point Likert scale (Strongly Disagree --- Strongly Agree) was used for the survey and data was collected using purposive sampling technique. A reliability analysis of the 20 items of the questionnaire was done to test for consistency, the Cronbach's alpha value was found to be 0.84.

The Independent variables for the study were celebrity types and product categories considered for the study while observations of respondents regarding influence of celebrity types on product categories was the dependent variable for the study.

Independent samples t-test was employed to test the hypotheses developed for the study.

4.0 Research Hypotheses

The following null and alternate hypotheses were developed for the purpose of study:

H1$_0$: Similar effectiveness of celebrity endorser types based on celebrity's professional life cycle have not been observed across product categories considered for the study

H1$_a$: Similar effectiveness of celebrity endorser types based on celebrity's professional life cycle have been observed on product categories considered for the study

H2$_0$: Similar effectiveness of celebrity endorser types based on their controversial nature have not been observed on product categories considered for the study

H2$_a$: Similar effectiveness of celebrity endorser types based on their controversial nature have been observed on product categories considered for the study

H3$_0$: Similar effectiveness of celebrity endorser types based on their country or origin have not been observed on product categories considered for the study

H3$_a$: Similar effectiveness of celebrity endorser types based on their country or origin have been observed on product categories considered for the study

H4$_0$: Similar effectiveness of celebrity endorser types based on their propensity to endorse multiple brands have not been observed on product categories considered for the study

H4$_a$: Similar effectiveness of celebrity endorser types based on their propensity to endorse multiple brands have been observed on product categories considered for the study

H5$_0$: Similar effectiveness of celebrity endorser types based on their nature of appearance in an endorsement have not been observed on product categories considered for the study

H5$_a$: Similar effectiveness of celebrity endorser types based on their nature of appearance in an endorsement have been observed on product categories considered for the study

5.0 Research Findings

Demographic Profile of Respondents (Gender)

- 71% of the respondents were male
- 29% of the respondents were female

Demographic Profile of Respondents (Age)

- 72% of the respondents were in the age bracket of 21-30 years

- 21% of the respondents were in the age bracket of 31- 40 years
- 7% of the respondents were in the age bracket of 41- 50 years

Demographic Profile of Respondents (Occupation)

- 53% of the respondents surveyed were Students
- 24% of the respondents surveyed were Service holders
- 21% of the respondents surveyed were Business people
- 2% of the respondents surveyed were Homemakers

5.1 Testing of Hypotheses

Hypothesis 1

H1$_0$: Similar effectiveness of celebrity endorser types based on celebrity's professional life cycle have not been observed across product categories considered for the study

$H1_0 : \mu \leq 3$

$H1_a$: Similar effectiveness of celebrity endorser types based on celebrity's professional life cycle have been observed across product categories considered for the study

$H1_a : \mu > 3$

An Independent samples t-test was undertaken to find out if similar influences of emerging and established celebrities (celebrity types based on celebrity life cycle in the profession pursued by the celebrity) on the product categories considered for the study were reported by respondents. The p value of which was found to be 0.001 (**Table 1.1**). Since the p value is less than 0.05 (p<0.05), we reject the null hypothesis and accept the alternate hypothesis $H1_a$ which states that **similar effectiveness of celebrity endorser** types based on celebrity's professional life cycle have been observed across product categories considered for the study..

Table 1.1: Independent Samples t-Test Conducted for H1

		Levene's Test for Equality of Variances		t-test for Equality of Means						
									95% Confidence Interval of the Difference	
		F	Sig.	t	df	Sig. (2-tailed)	Mean Difference	Std. Error Difference	Lower	Upper
H1	Equal variances assumed	5.907	.016	15.494	147	.001	1.51477	.09777	1.32156	1.70799
	Equal variances not assumed			14.315	68.643	.001	1.51477	.10581	1.30366	1.72589

Hypothesis 2

H2₀ : Similar effectiveness of celebrity endorser types based on their controversial nature have not been observed on product categories considered for the study

H2₀ : $\mu \leq 3$

H2ₐ : Similar effectiveness of celebrity endorser types based on their controversial nature have been observed on product categories considered for the study

H2ₐ : $\mu > 3$

An Independent samples t-test was undertaken to find out if similar influences of celebrity types based on their controversial nature (controversial vs non-controversial celebrities) on the product categories considered for the study were reported by respondents. The p value of which was found to be 0.001 (**Table 1.2**). Since the p value is less than 0.05 ($p<0.05$), we reject the null hypothesis and accept the alternate hypothesis **H2$_a$** which states that **similar effectiveness of celebrity endorser types based on their controversial nature have been observed on product categories considered for the study.**

Table 1.2: Independent Samples t-Test Conducted for H2

		Levene's Test for Equality of Variances		t-test for Equality of Means					95% Confidence Interval of the Difference	
		F	Sig.	t	df	Sig. (2-tailed)	Mean Difference	Std. Error Difference	Lower	Upper
H2	Equal variances assumed	.026	.873	15.300	147	.001	1.68923	.11041	1.47104	1.90742
	Equal variances not assumed			15.531	115.317	.001	1.68923	.10876	1.47379	1.90467

Hypothesis 3

H3₀ : Similar effectiveness of celebrity endorser types based on their country or origin have not been observed on product categories considered for the study

H3₀ : $\mu \leq 3$

H3ₐ : Similar effectiveness of celebrity endorser types based on their country or origin have been observed on product categories considered for the study

H3ₐ : $\mu > 3$

An Independent samples t-test was undertaken to find out if similar influences of celebrity types based on their country of origin (national vs foreign celebrities) on the product categories considered for the study were reported by respondents. The p value of which was found to be 0.001 (**Table 1.3**). Since the p value is less than 0.05 (p<0.05), we reject the null hypothesis and accept the alternate hypothesis **H3ₐ** which states that similar effectiveness of celebrity endorser types based on their country or origin have been observed on product categories considered for the study.

Table 1.3: Independent Samples t-Test Conducted for H3

		Levene's Test for Equality of Variances		t-test for Equality of Means					
								95% Confidence Interval of the Difference	
		F	Sig.	t	df	Sig. (2-tailed)	Mean Difference	Std. Error Difference	Lower	Upper
H3	Equal variances assumed	14.099	.000	17.035	147	.001	1.76273	.10348	1.55824	1.96723
	Equal variances not assumed			17.891	144.098	.001	1.76273	.09853	1.56799	1.95748

Hypothesis 4

H4₀ : Similar effectiveness of celebrity endorser types based on their propensity to endorse multiple brands have not been observed on product categories considered for the study

H4₀ : $\mu \leq 3$

H4ₐ : Similar effectiveness of celebrity endorser types based on their propensity to endorse multiple brands have been observed on product categories considered for the study

H4ₐ : $\mu > 3$

An Independent samples t-test was undertaken to find out if similar influences of celebrity types based on their propensity to endorse multiple brands (multiple brand endorsers vs single brand endorsers) on the product categories considered for the study were reported by respondents. The p value of which was found to be 0.001 (**Table 1.4**).

Since the p value is less than 0.05 (p<0.05), we reject the null hypothesis and accept the alternate hypothesis **H4$_a$** which states that **similar effectiveness of celebrity endorser types based on their propensity to endorse multiple brands have been observed on product categories considered for the study.**

Table 1.4: Independent Samples t-Test Conducted for H4

		Levene's Test for Equality of Variances		t-test for Equality of Means					95% Confidence Interval of the Difference	
		F	Sig.	t	df	Sig. (2-tailed)	Mean Difference	Std. Error Difference	Lower	Upper
H4	Equal variances assumed	.449	.504	16.136	147	.001	1.51169	.09369	1.32655	1.69984
	Equal variances not assumed			16.046	137.789	.001	1.51169	.09421	1.32541	1.69798

Hypothesis 5

$H5_0$: Similar effectiveness of celebrity endorser types based on their nature of appearance in an endorsement have not been observed on product categories considered for the study

$H5_0 : \mu \leq 3$

$H5_a$: Similar effectiveness of celebrity endorser types based on their nature of appearance in an endorsement have been observed on product categories considered for the study

$H5_a : \mu > 3$

An Independent samples t-test was undertaken to find out if similar influences of celebrity types based on their nature of appearance in an endorsement (celebrities appearing as themselves vs celebrities appearing in their fictional avatars) on the product categories considered for the study were reported by respondents. The p value of which was found to be 0.001 (**Table 1.5**). Since the p value is less than 0.05 ($p<0.05$), we reject the null hypothesis and accept the alternate hypothesis $H5_a$ which states that **similar effectiveness of celebrity endorser types based on their nature of appearance** in an endorsement have been observed on product categories considered for the study.

Table 1.5: Independent Samples t-Test Conducted for H5

	Levene's Test for Equality of Variances		t-test for Equality of Means						
								95% Confidence Interval of the Difference	
	F	Sig.	t	df	Sig. (2-tailed)	Mean Difference	Std. Error Difference	Lower	Upper
H5 Equal variances assumed	3.886	.051	17.066	147	.001	1.61568	.09467	1.42858	1.80278
Equal variances not assumed			17.569	142.956	.001	1.61568	.09196	1.43390	1.79747

6.0 Implications of the Study

The research study revealed certain interesting insights. It was observed that the following celebrity types - emerging, controversial, foreign origin, multiple brand endorsers and celebrities appearing as themselves in an endorsement were found to be ineffective in promoting brands as per the opinions shared by respondents. Matured celebrities were preferred across product categories considered for the survey and so were celebrities who were non-controversial, of Indian origin and those who were into single brand endorsements. However in the context of nature of appearance of a celebrity during endorsement, respondents preferred celebrities appearing as themselves rather than in their fictional avatars for pharmaceutical products. Probably transparency was the major aspect for convincing potential clients about a pharmaceutical product. This study should be helping marketers and advertisers to understand the type of celebrities who will be most effective as endorsers for FMCGs, consumer durables, pharmaceutical products and financial services. This study should also enable the consumer community to gain insights into the influence of celebrity types on product categories by appreciating the opinions shared by the respondents of the study.

7.0 Limitations of the Study

- Study was conducted in Kolkata only. If the study was simultaneously conducted in some of the other cities of the country, a more pan-Indian insight could have been gained through this study
- The demographic profile of the respondents was highly skewed

towards the male gender and the age bracket of 21-30 years. A more representation of the other demographic segments could have lent more credibility to the study
- More variety of celebrity endorser types could have been considered for the study
- More product categories could have been considered for the study

8.0 Conclusion

Celebrity endorsements have become one of the most potent weapons available with marketers today as far as brand building is concerned. Building credibility, improvising brand image, brand recall and brand acceptance and awareness are some of the major outcomes of brand endorsements. Hence it is absolutely necessary for marketers and advertisers to focus on proper celebrity selection so that effective selection of celebrities do complement and influence brands in a positive way and enable them to seek greater mileage in the overcrowded market space.

References
1. Agrawal, Pradeep and Dubey, S.K. (2012), "Celebrities: The Linking Pin Between Brands & Their Customer", *International Journal of Management & Business Studies*, 2(1), 56-60
2. Amos, Clinton, Holmes, Gary and Strutton, David (2008), "Exploring the relationship between celebrity endorser effects and advertising effectiveness", *International Journal of Advertising*, 27(2), 209-234
3. Chao, Paul, Wuhrer, Gerhard and Werani, Thomas (2005), "Celebrity and foreign brand name as

moderators of country-of-origin effects", *International Journal of Advertising",* 24(2), 173-192

4. Choi, Sejung Marina and Rifon, Nora J. (2012), "It Is a Match: The Impact of Congruence Between Celebrity Image and Consumer Ideal Self on Endorsement Effectiveness", *Psychology and Marketing,* 29(9), 639-650

5. Kim, H. and Park, S. Y. (2011), "Celebrity Endorsement in direct-to-consumer pharmaceutical advertising: the effects of celebrity-brand congruence and attributional inferences", *American Academy of Advertising Conference Proceedings*, 23-23

6. Lee, Jung-Gyo and Thorson, Esther (2008), "The Impact of Celebrity-Product Incongruence on the Effectiveness Of Product

Endorsement", *Journal of Advertising Research*, 48(3), 433-449

7. Parmar, J. Bhaveshkumar and Patel, P. Rajnikant (2014), "A Study on Consumer Perception for Celebrity & non-Celebrity Endorsement in Television Commercials for Fast Moving Consumer Goods", *Global Business and Economics Research Journal*, 3(2), 1-11

8. Rai, Naveen (2013), "Impact of Advertising on Consumer Behavior and Attitude with Reference To Consumer Durables", *International Journal of Management Research and Business Strategy"*, 2(2), 74-79

9. Silvera, David H and Austad, Benedikte (2004), "Factors predicting the effectiveness of celebrity endorsement advertisements",

European Journal of Marketing, 38(11/12), 1509-1526

10. Spilski, Anja and Klein, Andrea Groeppel (2008), "The Persistence of Fictional Character Images beyond the Program and their Use in Celebrity Endorsement: Experimental Results from a Media Context Perspective", *Advances in Consumer Research*, 35, 868-870

The Perceived Outcomes of Celebrity Endorsements

1.0 Introduction

The proliferation of brands and the competition on the market of goods and services have necessitated the usage of celebrity endorsements across the globe. Celebrity endorsements have become a prime brand communication strategy and this has aided the sale and promotion of goods and services across the globe (Nelson et al, 2012). Celebrity endorsement has been found to expedite brand image and purchase in most cases but then one important prerequisite for that is that the endorsement strategy needs to be backed by a powerful idea and effective positioning strategy.

The image of the endorsers has a direct impact on the image of the product being advertised as customers are often found to relate the celebrities to the products being advertised and although the success of endorsers in inducing sales is considered to be high; rarely are their impact on brands measured in terms of repeat sales when it comes to marketing practice. The appeal of a celebrity needs to be suitably blended with the image of the brand so that marketers can reap benefits out of an endorsement. Companies have been found to adopt celebrity endorsements as marketing strategy for the purpose of supporting corporate or brand imagery.

The present study discusses the various perceived outcomes of brand endorsements e.g. enhancement of image of the brands endorsed, triggering purchase intention among potential customers, facilitating brand association and recall etc. across demographic segments in Kolkata.

2.0 Literature Review

Celebrity endorsements are no different than other form of advertising as because it is driven by an idea and if the idea works well with the target audience, the endorsement will work too else it is doomed to be a failure (Woodward, 2006). The effectiveness of the technique is based on the fact that consumers often tend to feel that if a celebrity of their liking endorses a product then, it is the right product for them (Agrawal & Dubey, 2012).

In the contemporary marketing arena, celebrity endorsements have been considered as a preferred tool of advertising by several marketers and have been largely perceived as a winning formula for both product marketing and brand building (Patel, 2009). For marketers, it's a challenge to establish a strong association between a product and a celebrity because at the end of the day it endorsements are aimed at building brands and not build celebrities. There are certain pros and cons of endorsements. Some of the reasons why marketers go for celebrities are quick saliency, quick connect, quick means of brand differentiation and credibility.

Marketers worldwide have been found to rely on celebrity endorsements as they believe that such promotional tactics enhances brand awareness, brand equity and even financial returns. In the cosmetics industry, usage of celebrities to enhance brand loyalty has been observed to be a common place tactics (Lofgren & Li, 2010). Besides financial returns, marketers of cosmetic products have found that celebrity endorsements are a shortcut to gaining recognition for brands primarily which subsequently leads to generating brand loyalty. Both behavioral and attitudinal aspects and the relationship between them is to be taken into consideration while understanding the concept of brand loyalty being propagated through celebrity endorsements.

Celebrity endorsements across product categories have become a trend and are considered an effective tool for marketing of products and brand building (Mukherjee, 2009). It is easier to choose a celebrity than to establish a strong association between a product and its endorser. A certain relationship exists between celebrity endorsements and brands and between endorsements and consumer buying behavior and how consumers make brand preferences. Celebrity endorsements are to be considered a two-edged sword which is used effectively can offer benefits to brands else can backfire.

One among every four consumer profess to buy a product if it is endorsed by a celebrity and more than half of the consumers worldwide believe that a celebrity creates a distinct recognition or identity for a brand (Roberts, 2009). But then celebrities need to be used more strategically since almost every other brand now- a-days features a celebrity.

Celebrity endorsements do have a significant impact on customer perceptions and purchase intentions with respect to their physical attractiveness, source credibility and congruence (Zafar & Rafique, 2012). Celebrities have been found to draw customer attention in a cluttered marketing environment by exhibiting attributes like trustworthiness and likeability. The overall image of a celebrity along with the celebrity-product match has been found to enhance brand recall among customers. Endorsements have been found to enhance the sales of a company.

There are certain potential benefits of using celebrity endorsers and lot of studies have been conducted to analyze the impact of celebrity endorsement on advertising effectiveness. Celebrity endorsements offer certain tangible returns to marketers like building awareness for brands, making an emotional connect with the target audience, connecting quickly with the target group, inducing product usage among target group and building better brand image (Khatri, 2006).

The present study attempts to study the perceived outcomes of brand endorsements across various demographic variables considered for the survey and find out if any significant differences exist between various demographic segments of respondents as far as their opinions regarding effects of endorsements on brands are concerned.

3.0 Research Methodology

Based on literature review, the following outcomes of brand endorsements were identified and researched during the survey work – *enhancement of brand image, purchase intention, trial purchase, positive brand association, customer attention, brand recall, repeat purchase intention, attitude towards advertised brand, enhanced credibility of a brand and customer/audience engagement.* A sample size of

300 respondents from the city of Kolkata has been taken for the above mentioned purpose.

3.1 Hypotheses Formulation

Nelson et al (2012) find that celebrity endorsements backed by a powerful idea have been found to expedite brand image and purchase in most cases. Sonwalkar et al. (2011) confirm that celebrity endorsements play a major role in brand recall. Dhotre & Bhola (2010) observe in one of their research work that gender of respondents has no association with the recall for brands in the context of brand endorsements. Patra & Datta (2010) say that celebrity endorsements lead to projection of credible image for brands in terms of expertise, persuasiveness, trustworthiness and objectiveness. Lord & Putrevu (2009) mention that increased information credibility, enhancing customer attention and acceptance of a brand message and advantages related to positioning are some of the outcomes of celebrity endorsements. Escalas & Bettman (2009) find that celebrity endorsements have been found to enhance self-brand connections when consumers aspire to be like the celebrity. Marshall et al (2008) observe that customers often relate celebrities to products and endorsers are often considered successful in inducing sales of products and also repeat purchases of products. Rajakaski & Simonsson (2006) mention that celebrities make advertisements believable and enhance message recall. Khatri (2006) says that celebrity endorsements offer tangible returns to marketers like building awareness for brands, establishing an emotional connect with the target audiences, inducing product usage among them and building better brand image. Kamins et al (1989) observe that celebrity endorsement as a promotion strategy is found to attract customer attention towards brands advertised and lend credibility to advertisements featuring such brands. Several outcomes of celebrity endorsements have been reported by researchers in various literatures on celebrity endorsements but then are the reported outcomes similarly perceived by various demographic profiles of respondents? To probe this, the following null and alternate hypotheses are developed:

$H1_0$: Similar outcomes of celebrity endorsements have been reported across genders of respondents
$H1_a$: Similar outcomes of celebrity endorsements have not been reported across genders of respondents

$H2_0$: Similar outcomes of celebrity endorsements have been reported across age profiles of respondents

$H2_a$: *Similar outcomes of celebrity endorsements have not been reported across age profiles of respondents*

$H3_0$: *Similar outcomes of celebrity endorsements have been reported across occupations of respondents*
$H3_a$: *Similar outcomes of celebrity endorsements have not been reported across occupations of respondents*

3.2 Data Collection and Analysis

A total of 400 questionnaires were distributed to respondents for carrying out the survey in the city of Kolkata. 300 completed questionnaires were received back. Purposive sampling technique was used in the study for collection of data from the respondents in the city of Kolkata. The collected data has been analyzed through SPSS 19 (Statistical Package for Social Sciences Version 19). Statistical tools like Frequencies, Independent-samples T test and One-way ANOVA have been applied with the data.

4.0 Research Findings

The following pie charts give a vivid graphic description of the demographic profile of the respondents for the survey. For the purpose of the study, gender, age and occupation of the respondents were considered.

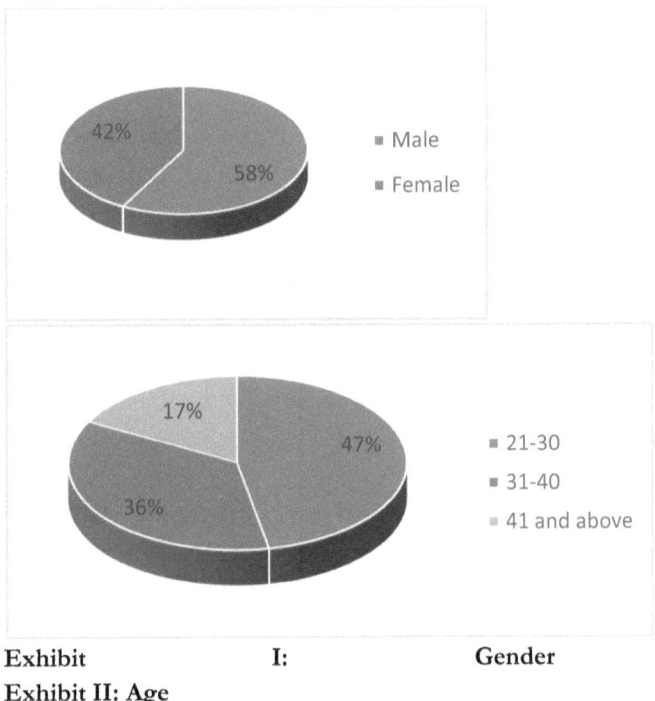

Exhibit I: Gender

Exhibit II: Age

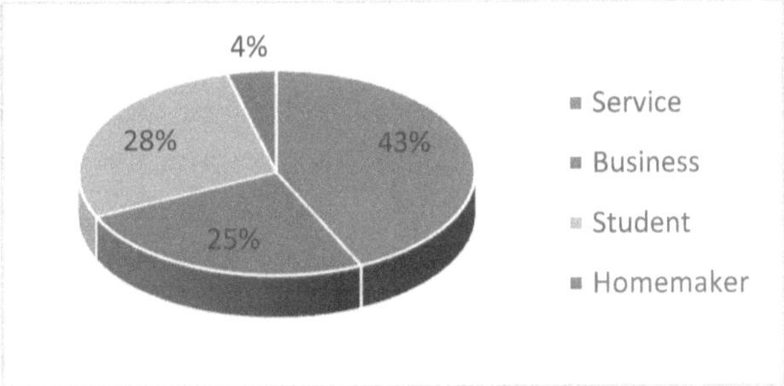

Exhibit III: Occupation

4.1 Hypotheses Testing
Hypothesis H1

The first hypothesis (H1) has been based on the assumption that similar outcomes of celebrity endorsements have been reported across genders of respondents. This has been hypothesized as follows-

H1$_0$: Similar outcomes of celebrity endorsements have been reported across genders of respondents
H1$_0$: $\mu > 3$

H1$_a$: Similar outcomes of celebrity endorsements have not been reported across genders of respondents
H1$_a$: $\mu \leq 3$

A two sample independent t test has been performed to test the above hypothesis. On the basis of responses obtained from the questionnaire, our null hypothesis is accepted in favor of the alternate hypothesis as the p value obtained is found to be more than 0.05 (p>0.05). Table 1.1 below presents the result of the two sample independent t test undertaken at 95% level of confidence.

Table 1.1: Reported Outcomes of Celebrity Endorsements Across Genders of Respondents

		Levene's Test for Equality of Variances		t-test for Equality of Means					95% Confidence Interval of the Difference	
		F	Sig.	t	df	Sig. (2-tailed)	Mean Difference	Std. Error Difference	Lower	Upper
MeanGender	Equal variances assumed	1.842	.176	.574	298	.566	.0513635	.0894229	-.1246168	.2273438
	Equal variances not assumed			.548	174.908	.585	.0513635	.0938088	-.1337794	.2365063

Since the null hypothesis is accepted in favor of the alternate hypothesis, it can be deduced that outcomes of celebrity endorsements are similarly reported across genders of respondents.

Hypothesis H2

The third main hypothesis (H2) has been based on the assumption that similar outcomes of celebrity endorsements have been reported across age profiles of respondents. This has been hypothesized as follows-

$H2_0$: Similar outcomes of celebrity endorsements have been reported across age profiles of respondents
$$\mu_1 = \mu_2 = \mu_3$$

$H2_a$: Similar outcomes of celebrity endorsements have not been reported across age profiles of respondents
$$\mu_1 \neq \mu_2 \neq \mu_3$$

A one way ANOVA test has been performed to test the above hypothesis. On the basis of responses obtained from the questionnaire, our null hypothesis is accepted as the p value obtained is found to be more than 0.05 ($p>0.05$). Table 1.2 below presents the result of the one way ANOVA test undertaken at 95% level of confidence.

Table 1.2: Reported Outcomes of Celebrity Endorsements Across Age Profiles of Respondents

	Sum of Squares	Df	Mean Square	F	Sig.
Between Groups	.296	2	.148	.277	.758
Within Groups	158.743	297	.534		
Total	159.039	299			

Since the null hypothesis is accepted, it can be deduced that outcomes of celebrity endorsements are similarly reported across age profiles of respondents.

Hypothesis H3

The third main hypothesis (H3) has been based on the assumption that similar outcomes of celebrity endorsements have been reported across occupations of respondents. This has been hypothesized as follows-

$H3_0$: *Similar outcomes of celebrity endorsements have been reported across occupations of respondents*
$\mu_1 = \mu_2 = \mu_3 = \mu_4$

$H3_a$: *Similar outcomes of celebrity endorsements have not been reported across occupations of respondents*
$\mu_1 \neq \mu_2 \neq \mu_3 \neq \mu_4$

A one way ANOVA test has been performed to test the above hypothesis. On the basis of responses obtained from the questionnaire, our null hypothesis is accepted as the p value obtained is found to be more than 0.05 ($p>0.05$). Table 1.3 below presents the result of the one way ANOVA test undertaken at 95% level of confidence.

Table 1.3: Reported Outcomes of Celebrity Endorsements Across Occupations of Respondents

	Sum of Squares	Df	Mean Square	F	Sig.
Between Groups	2.587	3	.862	1.632	.182
Within Groups	156.451	296	.529		
Total	159.039	299			

Since the null hypothesis is accepted, it can be deduced that outcomes of celebrity endorsements are similarly reported across occupations of respondents.

The above test results justify the contributions of the earlier researches which say that there are some tangible benefits for brands and their marketers as far as celebrity endorsements as a communication technique is concerned. Previous studies by Nelson et al (2012), Sonwalkar et al. (2011), Dhotre & Bhola (2010), Patra & Datta (2010), Lord & Putrevu (2009), Escalas & Bettman (2009), Rajakaski & Simonsson (2006), Khatri (2006), Kamins et al (1989) support this view. Moreover it is confirmed that outcomes of celebrity endorsements are similarly perceived and reported by respondents belonging to various demographic segments.

5.0 Implications of the Study

The present study highlights the fact that when it comes to perceived outcomes of brand endorsements, they are similarly reported across demographic segments of customers. No difference of opinion regarding any aspect of outcome related to brand endorsements were reported. This implies that marketers need to follow certain general guidelines for making potential customers aware, interested and engaged. The present study enables marketers to understand the elements which are of significant importance and to which they should be paying attention to while developing advertisements for brands featuring celebrities.

6.0 Limitations & Scope for further Research

The present study was conducted in Kolkata only. There could have been representation of few more demographic segments. Certain other aspects/outcomes of brand endorsements could have been considered.

The above said limitations do leave scope for further research in this area. A study can be conducted at a pan-India level with a greater sample size and more diverse representation of demographic profiles of informants. Further study on celebrity endorsements could throw up some more outcomes of endorsements that are of significance in general or in case of certain product categories which can be analyzed.

References

- Nelson, Okorie, Tunji, Oyedepo and Gloria, Akhidenor (2012), "The Dysfunctional and Functional Effect of Celebrity Endorsement on Brand Patronage", *Online Journal of Communication and Media Technologies*, 2(2), pp 141-152
- Woodward, David (2006), "You're a celebrity, get me out of this", *Director*, pp 58-60
- Agrawal, Pradeep and Dubey, S.K. (2012), "Celebrities: The Linking Pin Between Brands & Their Customer", *International Journal of Management & Business Studies*, 2(1), pp 56-60
- Patel, Pratik C. (2009), "Impact of Celebrity Endorsement on Brand Acceptance", The Icfai University Journal of Consumer Behavior, IV(1), pp 36-45
- Lofgren, Emma and Li, Juan (2010), "Brand Loyalty: A Study of the Prevalent Usage of Celebrity Endorsement in Cosmetics Advertising", www.diva-portal.org/smash/get/diva2:343717/FULLTEXT01.pdf

- Roberts, Jo (2009), "Don't just reach for the stars", *Marketing Week*, pp 20-22
- Zafar Qurat-Ul-Ain and Rafique Mahira (2012), "Impact of Celebrity Advertisement on Customers' Brand Perception and Purchase Intention", *Asian Journal of Business and Management Sciences*, 1(11), pp 53-67
- Khatri Puja (2006), "Celebrity Endorsement: A Strategic Promotion Perspective", *Indian Media Studies Journal*, 1(1), pp 25-37
- Sonwalkar Jayant, Kapse Manohar and Pathak Anuradha (2011), "Celebrity Impact – A Model of Celebrity Endorsement", *Journal of Marketing & Communication*, 7(1), pp 34-40
- Dhotre Meenal P. and Bhola Sarang S (2010), "Analytical Study of Association Between Celebrity Advertising and Brand Recall", *The IUP Journal of Brand Management*, VII (1 & 2), pp 25-50
- Patra Supriyo and Datta Saroj K. (2010), "Celebrity Endorsement in India- Emerging Trends and Challenges", 5(3), pp 16-23

- Lord Kenneth R. and Putrevu Sanjay (2009), "Informational and Transformational Responses to Celebrity Endorsements", *Journal of Current Issues and Research in Advertising*, 31(1), pp 1-13
- Escalas Jennifer Edson and Bettman James R. (2009), "Connecting with Celebrities: Celebrity Endorsement, Brand Meaning and Self-Brand Connections", *Journal of Marketing Research*, pp 1-35
- Rajakaski Johanna Jansson and Simonsson Regina (2006), "The Subject of Celebrity Endorsement: what it was and what it has become", *Bachelor Thesis on Marketing submitted at Lulea University of Technology*
- Kamins Michael A, Brand Meribeth J, Hoeke Stuart A and Moe John C (1989), "Two-Sided Versus One-Sided Celebrity Endorsements: The Impact on Advertising Effectiveness and Credibility", *Journal of Advertising*, 18(2), pp 4-10
- Mukherjee Debiprasad (2009), "Impact of Celebrity Endorsements on Brand Image", https://usdr.us/usdrinc/downloads/Celebrity-Endorsements.pdf

About the Author

Dr. Kisholoy Roy is a PhD in Management from IIT (Indian School of Mines), Dhanbad. He is a certified Accredited Management Teacher (AMT) who has been into teaching Management for several years now at the post graduate level. Dr Roy has authored several books on management apart from authoring various case studies, articles and research papers. He is presently engaged as an independent trainer and consultant in digital marketing and brand communication apart from his engagements as a faculty in Marketing with various B-schools.

www.ingramcontent.com/pod-product-compliance
Lightning Source LLC
Chambersburg PA
CBHW020652220526
45464CB00001B/405